THRIFT STORE
SHOES
A MEMOIR

to Janet —
Many blessings
Connie Lounsbury
2013

Also by Connie Lounsbury

QUIT YOUR JOB AND MAKE ENDS MEET
Published by Communication Spectrum
(out of print)

REACHING PAST THE WIRE: A NURSE AT ABU GHRAIB
Published by Borealis Books

THRIFT STORE SHOES

A MEMOIR

CONNIE LOUNSBURY

Inspiring Voices
A Service of Guideposts

Inspiring Voices books may be ordered through booksellers or by contacting:

Inspiring Voices
1663 Liberty Drive
Bloomington, IN 47403
www.inspiringvoices.com
1-(866) 697-5313

Because of the dynamic nature of the Internet, any web addresses or
links contained in this book may have changed since publication and
may no longer be valid. The views expressed in this work are solely those
of the author and do not necessarily reflect the views of the publisher,
and the publisher hereby disclaims any responsibility for them.

ISBN: 978-1-4624-0035-5 (e)
ISBN: 978-1-4624-0036-2 (sc)

Library of Congress Control Number: 2011943846

Printed in the United States of America

Inspiring Voices rev. date: 12/12/2011

To my husband, David—

The finest man I've ever known

My abundant thanks to
Vicki Williamson, Connie Lee,
and
Darlene Anderson,
my wonderful, insightful, Christian friends,
who worked tirelessly with me in my edits.

CONTENTS

PREFACE

I am enormously grateful to God for the grace He has shown me during these seventy years of my life. In the rules of golf, each player is allowed one do-over without penalty when they mess up. The free do-over is called a "mulligan." In my game of life, God has allowed me more than one mulligan. I have been slow to listen to how God wants me to live and have, consequently, made many mistakes and have many regrets.

But God has continued to love me and bless me abundantly with a wonderful family and many friends. Those are the most important blessings we can ever hope to receive.

And so my life continues in God's grace.

CHAPTER ONE

THE FIRE

We still talk about that frigid January morning in 1950, when I was nine years old. It was the last Saturday of our Christmas vacation from school, and my older brother, Lee, my three younger sisters, and I slept late. We quickly dressed in the cold and rushed downstairs to the warmth of the roaring fire in the wood stove that sat in the middle of the living room. It was the only source of heat in that old, rented farmhouse near Orrock, Minnesota.

We kids all huddled close to the stove. Mom was in the kitchen cooking oatmeal. I was brushing my hair, and Lee squatted on the other side of the stove, tying his shoelaces. "Don't stand so close to the stove, Irene," I said to my youngest sister. "You might get burned."

"I'm cold," Irene said.

"Come and stand in front of me," I told her. "Then your back will be warm too."

The door opened, and Dad came in with an armload of wood crusted with snow and ice. Cold air blew into the room, and we all shivered. "We'll need a lot of wood to keep the house warm today," Dad said as he stacked the wood behind the stove.

Mom called from the kitchen, "Bob! Something's wrong upstairs. It sounds like marbles rolling across the floor. Go see."

Dad walked past us, opened the door, and started up the stairs. "Fire!" he yelled. His heavy feet raced back down. "The house is on fire! Get the kids out!"

"Lee, Connie, help me with the girls," Mom yelled as she grabbed coats, hats, and mittens from the hooks by the door. "Take them to Schaufield's. Tell them to call the fire department and come help us."

I looked at the bobby pins gripped in my left hand and the hairbrush held in my right hand. I needed to put them somewhere. *Let go of them. But where?*

"Hurry, Connie," Mom yelled. "Come help." Her words brought me to my senses. I dropped everything and ran to her.

As I helped Donna with her coat, hat, and mittens, Dad threw a radio and some chairs into the snow bank from the open doorway next to me. I heard thumps and bangs as things hit the floor upstairs. The smell of smoke became strong. "Come too," I pleaded as Mom pushed us out the door.

"I have to get things out," she said. "Run fast!" As we left the house, she yelled to Dad, "Get the sewing machine!"

The cold morning air stung my face as we ran down the driveway to the road. Lee carried Judie, I carried Irene, and Donna hung on to my coat as we ran through the snow. I had forgotten to put on my winter boots and the snow and subzero temperatures seeped through my open-toed shoes and anklets. Soon I could no longer taste the salt from my tears because the frigid air crusted them on my cheeks.

At the end of the driveway, I turned and looked back at the house. Dark gray smoke seeped out from under the roof, and I heard the crackling of wood. Mom's sewing machine sat tilted in the snow among other scattered items a short distance from the house. After we got around the curve in the road, Irene's weight in my arms prevented me from turning to look again, so I kept running.

Mr. and Mrs. Schaufield lived only a short distance across the road, but when we got there, they weren't home. "They're probably milking cows at Grandpa Schaufield's," Lee said.

No one locked doors in rural Minnesota in the 1950s. We could have walked into the warmth and safety of their home. But we knew better than to go into someone's house uninvited, so we began to walk to Grandpa Schaufield's farm. I could no longer feel my toes.

I heard windows exploding and looked back toward our house. Dark, angry, black smoke rose high into the air, and bright orange flames shot out of the window of the upstairs bedroom I shared with Donna and Judie. I squeezed my eyes closed against the image of our beds and clothes being burned. *Mom! Dad!* "Father in Heaven," I whispered to myself. "Help them! Keep Mom and Dad safe."

I shifted Irene's weight in my arms and ran faster to catch up with Lee. When I did, both Lee and I stopped, put the girls down, and rested our arms. Irene was three and Judie was five. In only a few moments, we continued in a slow, jerky jog. None of us talked except Donna, who pleaded to be carried.

Later Mrs. Schaufield said they had heard what they thought were calves bawling when they saw all five of the Duncan children coming down the driveway crying: "The two oldest carrying the two youngest; a mile down the road behind them, a thick cloud of smoke telling their sad story."

All four of the Schaufields ran to meet us. Grandma Schaufield picked up Donna; Grandpa took Irene from me, and Mr. Schaufield took Judie from Lee. They ushered us into the warmth of the kitchen and took off our coats and hats. I sat as if deaf and dumb. Lee stood by the door refusing to remove his coat and cap, even after Mr. and Mrs. Schaufield and Grandpa went to our burning house without him. "Mom and Dad need me," he kept saying. "They need me."

Grandma stayed with us, and took off my shoes and frozen stockings, and put my feet into a pan of warm water. Lee moved to the stove but refused to remove his coat. Irene climbed onto my lap, and Donna and Judie sat on the floor close to me. Nothing seemed real. I felt as if I were looking at myself from outside my body—not feeling anything, just observing. Then the pins and needles began prickling my feet as they began to thaw.

Mr. Schaufield soon brought Mom to us. She smelled of bitter smoke. Soot and tears streaked her face. Her hands shook as she held Irene tightly on her lap. "My saddle?" Lee asked. "My fishing rod? Did you get them out? They were upstairs."

"Everything upstairs burned," Mom said, her voice breaking.

Lee turned away and cried, his face against the door, thin shoulders jerking inside his jacket. I cried for him too. He had trapped gophers all summer for the fifteen-cents-per-tail bounty, and he had saved his money to buy that rod and reel. The saddle, a recent birthday gift from Uncle Marsh, the man who had raised Dad, was old and scruffy, but Lee cherished it as if it were new. He hadn't even used it yet.

"I got your Tinkertoys out," Mom added. Santa had brought them just a couple weeks earlier. I wondered about my own Christmas gift—a rag doll wearing a dress of the same flower-sack fabric as the pajamas that Mom had made for Donna a few months earlier. My clothes were of more concern. Mom had made me two new dresses for school this year. They were upstairs.

Later, when Dad and the men came back from putting out the final flames of our home, Dad stood by the door, his cap in his hand, his eyes apologetic. He and Mom were only able to pull out family photographs, Mom's treadle sewing machine, and a few other personal belongings before flames consumed the house. "It's not your fault," I wanted to say. But here stood a man who never did well enough for his family to begin with, who had now lost all the possessions he had ever accumulated. We had no insurance. Unemployed, unable to replace anything we had lost, he looked like an accused criminal who no longer believed in his own innocence.

Dad took off his coat but kept his eyes downcast. He accepted coffee with a nod of thanks and sat at the kitchen table with shoulders slumped, saying nothing as he lifted his cup with trembling hands. Our strong, handsome father had become a tired, sad, old man.

What will become of us?

CHAPTER TWO

MOM

My shock at having everything I owned suddenly gone turned to grief when I thought of moving again. It had been a good year at that farm in Orrock. Now, once again, I'd be the new girl at school, living in a different house and a different town. This time the reason wasn't because Dad "has gypsy blood," as Mom often said, but it still meant another change.

I had loved my little country school—where grades one through eight sat together in one room and were taught by one teacher, Mrs. Florence Lundsten. I shared the third and part of the fourth grade with Karen Woolhouse and Ethel Lemon at Kragaro School where we began each day by reciting the Pledge of Allegiance. I sat near the front, so I could see the blackboard and the roll-down maps. I didn't want to miss anything.

We had rows of wooden desks with lift-up tops. Mrs. Lundsten frequently interrupted her teaching to put wood into the stove at the rear of the room, our only source of heat. The smell of smoke competed with the smell of wet coats, scarves, and mittens hanging in the back cloakroom near the entrance. When we needed a restroom, we went behind the schoolhouse, in the cold and snow, to the outhouse—one side for the boys and the other for the girls.

Mrs. Lundsten made learning fun. All eight grades of her students took turns reading from a book every morning. I've never forgotten the Little House on the Prairie series, especially *The Long Winter.*

Mrs. Lundsten was so much more than just a schoolteacher to us students. She seemed to first sense, and then meet, all our needs. When Lee stuttered, Mrs. Lundsten taught him to sing his words, so he could make a sentence. Lee was embarrassed to sing until he learned that doing so enabled him to communicate quickly and easily, without stuttering.

Mrs. Lundsten took Lee and me on a train trip one day because we had never been on one. We didn't go far, but it was an exhilarating experience. The other kids at school accused me of being "teacher's pet," and after that treat, I thought maybe it was true. But I didn't mind.

At the beginning of fourth grade, Jerry Woolhouse told me I was his girlfriend. He was a year older than me. I liked Jerry too and was grieved when he was diagnosed with a brain tumor. He missed a lot of school and died shortly thereafter. I was inconsolable.

Our parents did not plan to attend the funeral, so Mrs. Lundsten took Lee and me to the funeral. I had never seen a dead person before, and his white, stonelike face scared me. He didn't look like himself. I cried into Mrs. Lundsten's tan coat sleeve. She let me cry for a while, then gently took her sleeve from me, and put both arms around me and held me close to her so I could cry some more. I loved Mrs. Lundsten.

Forty-nine years after that funeral, my mother died in 1999. I found a letter from Mrs. Lundsten tucked away in Mom's small box of important papers. It merely asked Mom to have us at the school at a certain time so we could leave with her for Jerry's funeral.

Why did Mom keep that letter as one of her treasures? She had so few things in that box. I can only believe, as a teacher and a person of education, Mrs. Lundsten's letter to Mom probably compared to my autograph of Harry Belafonte.

Mom also admired Mrs. Lundsten because this teacher gave us raisins for a snack at recess, and frequently simmered goulash on the wood stove, and served all her students a hot noon meal. She always dished out an especially generous serving to Kenny Johnson whose mother had died.

Did she also have Lee and me in mind when she fed her students? Dad drove truck in the city for a while that year and came home on weekends to farm our few rented acres, but he was often unemployed. Times were tough. We only ate lavishly on the Sundays when my uncle Chester, aunt Ruth, and cousins Ruthie and Alvin came to visit us.

"Sunday is a day of rest," Dad always declared. Then the men and boys loaded up the fishing gear, drove to a lake, rented a rowboat, and fished until noon.

On that same "day of rest" my mother took the hatchet out of the woodshed and propped it against the chopping block before she walked into the chicken coop for our dinner. Of everything on the farm, Mom loved her chickens the most. Mom wasn't one to "neighbor" much, and sometimes I thought she liked talking to her chickens more than she liked talking to us children. Maybe in the chicken coop, away from earshot of her children, she voiced thoughts and feelings she couldn't voice anywhere else.

Every day she dipped her right hand into the gray galvanized pail she cradled in her left arm and pulled out a handful of ground corn. Then, she slowly walked round and round that pen flicking feed onto the ground with her long, bony wrist as she talked to the chickens. "We need rain, yes we do. Or we won't get a good crop this year." On and on she talked until the pail was empty.

She gathered the eggs herself too, even though Lee and I were old enough to have that chore. She'd say, "I'm going to the henhouse now, Connie. Watch the girls." She picked eggs from all the nests and even reached under the brood hens that didn't want to give up their future family, talking gently to the chickens all the while.

So when she walked into that pen, scooped up a big fat chicken, laid it on the chopping block and, with one swift hatchet stroke, saw the bird's head roll off onto the ground, it was hard to understand. She loved those chickens. Sometimes the chicken rolled off the block and ran wildly in circles, blood spurting out of its severed neck, until it fell.

She then held the chicken by its legs, neck downward, until it bled out. Mom plucked the feathers and singed the pinfeathers over the flame on the kitchen stove. She gutted the chicken, washed it thoroughly, and cut it into small enough pieces to serve eleven people. When the fishermen came home, Mom had a dinner prepared of crispy fried chicken, mashed potatoes, gravy, and whatever vegetable proved ready in her garden.

She did what was necessary. I always thought of Mom as being weak. I think I misjudged her.

"Save the neck for me," Mom said as she passed the platter of chicken around the table. It was the only piece left when the platter came back to her.

Several years ago, after my mother had died, cousin Ruthie showed me an old black-and-white photo that her mother had taken of our family on one of those Sundays. I looked at the photo of my parents posed in front of my uncle's new, black, 1950 Studebaker. We five children stood in front of them. My eyes darted to each of us in the photo, but focused on Mom. She was so skinny! Her hair was unkempt—so unlike her. She wore an apron over her housedress as if she had been summoned from the kitchen to pose for the picture. She wasn't smiling. She always hated having her picture taken.

Dad was in his usual blue chambray shirt, sleeves rolled up to the elbows, a round spot worn thin on his breast pocket where he always carried a box of Copenhagen snuff. The bill on his baseball cap tilted upward, his smiling face as handsome as I remembered.

Lee was grinning. Barefoot, freckle-faced, wearing bib overalls without a shirt, he looked like he could have stepped out of a Mark Twain novel. Donna, Judie, and Irene all wore shy smiles and what looked like handmade dresses. And there was me, the oldest daughter—mother's helper. I looked so serious, so grown up already. My first pair of glasses, blonde hair in a ponytail, I was holding Irene's hand. Always the caretaker.

My eyes returned to Mom in the picture. She would have been thirty years old. Her flowered housedress hung on her tall, bony frame. *Save me the neck of the chicken!* That memory came to me like a flash. It made me wonder how often my mother fed us first and ate only what was left.

A weak mother? How could I have thought that?

I never went hungry. Sometimes only a slice of homemade bread spread with lard and sprinkled with salt was available to us, but it was filling, and we actually learned to like it. Mom used her coffee grounds so many times that sometimes her coffee had hardly any color to it by the time Dad came home on Friday evening with groceries—when he had a job. I learned very young that we didn't have money for things that many other people had, like store-bought clothes, cookies, or books.

Mom's life never got much better. Dad died when she was only 58. After Mom had a stroke in her seventies, she came to live with my husband and me. She asked me once why we didn't raise chickens since we had a farm. I think she would have loved to see chickens again—maybe even feed the chickens.

Was I good enough to her when she was with us? I don't think so. She sacrificed so much for me as a child, yet I sometimes resented the sacrifices I had to make to fit her into our small home. Now, with all my heart I want her back—even for a week. I'd go out and buy a few Rhode Island Red hens and a rooster so she could talk to them. I'd cook her favorite pot roast and bake chocolate brownies for her again. We'd talk all day and then I'd take her to play bingo. I'd rub lotion on her back again, using my lavender lotion that she loved so much, polish her toenails, and dote on her.

My mother deserved it.

CHAPTER THREE
LIFE AT ORROCK

Those hours after the fire, as I grieved over what I would miss at Orrock, I knew I wouldn't miss feeding and watering Dad's two workhorses. When Dad had a job in the city, as he had all that past summer, Lee and I cared for the horses. Feeding them was okay. Lee hefted the heavy hay bales and I measured out the oats and put them in the feed bunks. Watering wasn't as easy.

We pumped water to fill a five-gallon pail. We both held the handle—one on each side—and carried the pail from the pump to the barn, a long distance when your burden is almost bigger than you. The worst part was getting to the horse with the water and watching him draw up the whole pail in three long draughts—and want more. And we had two horses. Even though I wore heavy gloves, my hands hurt long afterward from the wire handle of the heavy pail.

On cold winter mornings we sometimes had to thaw the frozen pump with kettles of boiling water before we began pumping. We did this before we walked to school in the morning and again before supper. No, I wouldn't miss watering horses. I hoped Dad wouldn't rent another farm or bring the horses with us.

I hoped in our next move we would live close to another girl my age. I desperately wanted a girlfriend to share my secrets, to write stories and braid hair together, and to talk about the books we read in school. No one my age ever came to our house and we never went anywhere.

Now, when I think about my loneliness, I can't help but wonder about Mom. She didn't have a friend, either. She had no one to visit with, and no one to share her secrets with either. No wonder she spent so much time with her chickens. At least she could talk to them, even if they didn't answer back.

Sometimes I couldn't hold in my loneliness and the tears flowed. I learned to cry silently at night so that I didn't upset my sisters. They had their own world. They had each other. Lee, who was eleven, had his chores, but after that he was free to do whatever he wanted. He never included me. Who wanted to hunt squirrels with a slingshot or trap gophers anyway? My sisters were six, five, and three—too young to share in the kind of fun I, at nine, wanted—or to understand the things I longed to talk about with a girlfriend. Instead, I felt more like a mother than a child.

I was always in charge of caring for my sisters while Mom did her housework, sewing, cooking, baking, and gardening. Mom made all our clothes from others' castoffs or from the fabric sacks in which flour was sold.

Mom canned vegetables from the garden and picked wild chokecherries. She canned the juice so she could make jelly when she could afford the sugar. She picked apples when someone allowed her to pick from their tree, and picked wild blueberries and canned blueberry sauce. Mom was always working at providing food and clothing for us. Since she needed me to help her, I rarely had time for myself.

While I longed for a friend of my own, my "mother's helper" status earned me compliments from my mother. Therefore, I strived to be even more helpful. Reading was my passion, but we had no books at home, so I made up my own stories and told them to my sisters. I also took them on walks in the woods, played house with them, and watched to make sure they didn't get hurt or into any trouble. No matter where we lived, my job was always "mother's helper." That's why I mattered. But I longed to matter just because I was me.

Why, when I was so passionate about reading, didn't I become more vocal about wanting books? Did I take my cue from Mom, who quietly accepted things as they were, never complaining or asking for more? I also didn't know that anyone else had books at home to read. We didn't visit other people's homes. But, oh, how I longed for books of my own to read.

For the Christmas program at school a few weeks earlier, we had spent most of Thursday afternoon cutting and pasting decorations for the tall Christmas tree that crowded into the front corner of the one-room schoolhouse. I made red hearts, white angels, and blue snowballs. I stood in front of the tree that afternoon and counted twenty-three tree decorations that were mine.

"You did an excellent job," Mrs. Lundsten said and patted my shoulder. I'm sure my face glowed. *I did an excellent job*—Mrs. Lundsten said so.

The evening before our Christmas vacation from school began, the parents came to see us perform a Christmas program. Even Mom and Dad were there. We almost didn't make it because it was a very cold night and Dad's car didn't want to start. Just when I was getting nervous about being late, the car finally roared to life. We could see our breath in the air, but having all four of us oldest children crowded in the back helped to keep us warm on our ride to school, only a couple miles away.

I was eager for everyone to see our beautiful Christmas tree. I wore a new dress that Mom had made that fall, and Mom curled my long, blonde hair with the curling iron heated on the wood stove. My curls bounced when I walked and I kept turning my head to make them bounce even more. Although I was smiling, my stomach felt the way Mom's coffee pot bubbled when it began percolating. I would soon have to perform my part in the play and remember the words to many songs.

Mrs. Lundsten gave even Donna a small part since she would start first grade the following year. She looked so cute standing in front reciting her piece in a singsong voice while she made circles on the floor with one foot. We did a short play of the birth of Baby Jesus. I was an angel, complete with wings that Mrs. Lundsten had made. We sang "Away in a Manger," "O Little Town of Bethlehem," "and Silent Night." Then the chairman of the school board gave each child a brown paper bag filled with salted peanuts in the shell, hard Christmas candy, and an orange. What a treat, especially the huge piece of ribbon candy in my bag that my brother envied. His piece of ribbon candy was much smaller. I kept him envious for several days before I shared part of my candy with him.

The country school had been wonderful, but what I would miss the most, I decided, was going to Sunday school with the Hanson family.

CHAPTER FOUR

GOING TO CHURCH

Sometimes the smallest incident changes our lives, but we know that only as we look backward. A single thing, such as a stranger driving down the dusty, gravel road to our farmhouse late that previous summer, changed the course of my life.

He pulled up and parked near the house. I was swinging on our old tree swing, a few feet from where my sisters played in a tractor-tire sandbox. The tall, friendly-looking man in a suit and tie got out of his car and waved to me. I waved back. He walked fast and went right up to the door. Seconds after he knocked, my mother opened the screen.

Because I couldn't hear from there, I got out of the swing and crept forward. He was telling Mom that he and his family lived just north of us and they attended a church in the country nearby. "We'd sure like to have you folks visit," he said. I liked the kindness in his deep voice.

"Thank you," my mother said.

"It's a great church." He told her about the people and the activities. "I'm sure you and your family would enjoy worshiping with us."

Mom smiled at him without comment. He waved to me again as he drove away.

I had never been to church, but now I would know what my friends talked about. I could hardly wait for Sunday. When I asked Mom about attending, she said, "We're not going."

"Why not? I want to go."

"I don't have anything decent to wear," Mom said and turned back to her ironing. By the set look on her face I knew the subject was closed.

The following week the man drove into our yard again. He stopped to greet Lee and admire his slingshot before walking up to the door to talk to Mom. "My wife and I—and our daughter, Sandra—would like to stop by next Sunday morning and drive you and your family to church."

"You're very kind," Mom said, "but that won't be necessary."

The man glanced at me standing next to Mom. I couldn't keep the disappointment from showing on my face. "Perhaps we could bring your two oldest children. They're the right age to attend Sunday school." He smiled at me in such a friendly way that I grinned back at him.

Mom paused for a moment. She looked at me. I nodded vigorously. She gazed past the man in the open doorway to where Lee stood shooting stones into a tree. "I guess that would be okay," she said.

I breathed a sigh of relief. As soon as the man left, I ran out to tell Lee the good news. "Why do we have to go to Sunday school?" he asked.

"Because Mom said so," I retorted, falling back on Mom's pat answer to most of my questions. I didn't want him to do or say anything to ruin my chance of going to Sunday school.

Times were more innocent back in 1951. People trusted each other. So that's how it came about that Mr. and Mrs. Hanson and their daughter Sandra—the neighbors we didn't know—picked us up and drove Lee and me to church and Sunday school the next Sunday.

He drove to a little white church that wasn't much bigger than our schoolhouse, but it had a tall bell tower and a large front staircase. Mr. Hanson parked his car alongside several others, and Lee and I got out of the back seat along with Sandra, who was a few years older than we were. Mrs. Hanson took my hand and we all walked up those many steps together. I turned my head a couple times to make sure Lee was still with us. He didn't appear very happy at being dressed in his school clothes, attending church instead of checking his gopher traps or going fishing. I felt sorry that he wasn't as excited as I was.

I was relieved to see several kids we knew from school. Everybody knew the Hanson family and greeted them by name. Mr. and Mrs. Hanson introduced Lee and me to people we didn't know. Many adults shook our hands and welcomed us like they were really happy to see us there. The preacher squeezed my hand so tight that it hurt. I didn't like him much.

A round wood stove sat toward the back of the church. A man opened the door and put a few pieces of wood into the already hot fire. I smelled coffee and saw a large coffee pot on top of the stove. *They drink coffee in church?*

After a bit of standing around talking, we walked toward the front of the church and sat on long, wooden benches. Mrs. Hanson had explained that we would first hear a sermon and then we would go to Sunday school classes.

The preacher was a tall, thin man with a high-pitched voice that was unpleasant to listen to. My mind kept wandering away from what he was saying. I was happy when the sermon and singing ended so we could go to Sunday school. However, instead of going to classes, everyone gathered toward the back of the church to drink coffee and lemonade, eat cookies, and talk to each other. I frowned when I saw Lee take a second cookie. Mom wouldn't have been proud of him. He saw my frown and stuck his tongue out at me.

I was happy when Mrs. Hanson said it was time to go to the front corner of the room where both third-and-fourth-graders met. Lee and I would be in the same class. I liked that because I felt responsible for Lee being there and I wanted him to be happy. Some of his rowdy school friends were in that class, so he goofed around with them and seemed okay.

When I told Mrs. Hanson how much I enjoyed Sunday school, she said they would take us to church every week. After that, I eagerly waited for each Sunday to arrive. I loved being with Mr. and Mrs. Hanson. They held my hand when we walked across the parking lot, and Mrs. Hanson even hugged me once when I showed her a Sunday school paper where I had answered all the questions right. Mom and Dad never showed affection to us like that.

I adored my Sunday school teacher, a soft-spoken, beautiful woman with long, thick, dark, curly hair—so unlike my fine, straight, blonde hair. She told us about Jesus and how he loves little children. She read Bible stories to us about David and Goliath, Moses in the bulrushes, and my favorite—the fiery furnace of Shadrach, Meshach and Abednego.

Lee especially liked the story of David and Goliath. One day I saw him pull back hard on the black tire rubber that Dad had attached to the Y of a tree branch for his slingshot. As he did so, he said, "The Mighty Leroy slays the giant!"

I looked closely at my brother. His light brown hair stuck up like a rooster tail in the back, yet the front fell forward onto his freckled face. Barefoot, faded blue bib overalls, no shirt—his skinny arms nonetheless showed big muscle bulges as he pulled back for another shot. *Mighty Leroy?* Yes. He was mighty in my eyes. If a giant did appear, I knew he would stand between us and fight with all his might.

My brother was my hero.

CHAPTER FIVE

BILLY GRAHAM

After Thanksgiving Mr. and Mrs. Hanson invited us to go to Minneapolis with them to hear the young evangelist Billy Graham speak. I pleaded with Mom until she gave her permission. When she said we could go, I should have known better, but I went running to Lee. "Guess what? Guess what?" I yelled before I even reached him. "We get to go to Minneapolis to hear somebody speak. Mr. Hanson asked Mom and she said yes."

Lee glared at me and ran to the house. "Why do I have to go just because Connie wants to go?" he whined to Mom.

"Because you're her big brother and you need to take care of her," Mom said. I had followed Lee to the house, worried Mom would change her mind. My relief when she didn't was partly spoiled when Lee stayed mad at me for several days.

The big day to see Billy Graham arrived cold and snowy. The trip from our home to Minneapolis was long, but I was transfixed as I watched scenery out the car window. Trees, farms, houses, cars, people, cows, horses, sheep, chickens, dogs, and cats whizzed past my side window. As I stored it all in my mind and eagerly awaited what might pass my vision next, I saw big rivers and small streams. Someone had a big, white goat in a barnyard. Sandra, who sat in the middle, taught Lee some games with her fingers. *This is the church. This is the steeple. Open the door and see all the people.*

The closer we got to Minneapolis, the faster everyone moved. I felt dizzy watching so many people and cars and trucks moving at such a high speed. *Don't they crash into each other sometimes?* Sandra was trying to guess which of Lee's hands held the marble.

We arrived at our destination. Mr. Hanson parked the car and we walked into a huge building—I can't remember whether it was a church or an auditorium. We found seats a long way from the stage. Mr. Hanson helped me remove my coat. He tucked my mittens and hat into one of the sleeves. "So you don't lose them," he told me as he draped the coat over the back of my seat. Lee took off his coat and did the same thing. Many people were already seated. Others were just arriving. The room was full of music and talking.

People on stage played the piano, drums, and other instruments that I didn't recognize. Others—Sandra later said they were a choir—sang songs. We had songbooks too, and when we were supposed to sing, I sang loudly along with more people than I had ever seen in one place. I stood between Lee and Mr. Hanson and enjoyed the rich sound of Mr. Hanson's voice as he sang with joy.

Lee looked bored and didn't sing, but others in the room seemed as if they loved being there and loved each other. I felt so warm and wonderful in the midst of all that happiness that I couldn't stop smiling. I smiled at Lee. He started to frown, but gave me a small grin instead. He didn't hate it as much as he wanted me to believe he did.

Billy Graham came onto the stage. Everyone became quiet. His voice was strong and powerful. He prayed and we prayed with him. I am certain he spoke eloquently about many things, but I heard only this simple message directed to me: "You have a Father in Heaven who loves you very much."

Those words rang through my head again and again. *Two fathers?* I couldn't believe I had *two* fathers. I wasn't sure my dad loved me. When he was home he stayed busy doing things that didn't include me. He rarely spoke to me, so I didn't know how he felt about me. But Billy Graham said that my Father in Heaven loved me. *How could that be possible?*

"Your Father in Heaven will always be there for you," Mr. Graham said. My dad was never there for me. He was at work a lot, and when he was home he was either fixing the car, caring for the horses, or working in the fields. Once when I asked Dad a question, he gave me an answer. But when I used that information in school, it was incorrect. Dad had only gone to school through the eighth grade and he was wrong about a lot of things. For instance, he didn't believe the world was round. I had decided long ago to not rely on my father.

"Your Father in Heaven will forgive your sins and make you pure again."

As I listened, I thought about my sins. My Sunday school teacher said stealing and lying were sins. I stole one of Mom's cigarettes and tried to smoke it behind the barn with my cousin when I was six. Once I ate all four of the cookies Mom gave me, instead of sharing with my sisters like Mom instructed. Sometimes I lied to my mother when I really hadn't brushed my hair a hundred strokes before I went to bed. Sometimes I lied to Lee to get him to do what I wanted him to do. Mr. Graham said I could say "I'm sorry" and my Father in Heaven would forgive me.

"If you are lonely, you can talk to your Father in Heaven. He will listen to you."

My dad didn't listen to me. When he came into the house at the end of the day, he was too tired to listen to me.

My mother was busy cooking, cleaning, washing, sewing or ironing clothes, working in the garden, canning fruits and vegetables, or caring for the little girls. She rarely listened to me. I had no books to read and no playmates, and I felt lonely most of the time. It would be nice to have someone who would listen to me.

"Your Father in Heaven will love and protect you."

I didn't feel loved or protected and I wanted to, more than anything.

Billy Graham asked us to come down to the front to say yes—to claim the Father in Heaven as our own. I wanted to claim that Father in Heaven.

As the congregation sang "Just as I Am," people left their seats and walked down the aisles to where Billy Graham stood. The rest of us sang that song over and over again. My heart was so filled with the spirit of love and hope and the desire to have this wonderful Father for myself that I was overcome with tears.

Mr. Hanson leaned down to me. "Do you want to go to the front, Connie?" I was crying so hard I could only nod. He gave me his handkerchief. I blew my nose and gave the handkerchief back to him. He took my hand and led me down the aisle along with hundreds of others. Lee gave me a surprised look when I got up, but I ignored him.

At the altar, Mr. Graham asked me if I believed in the Lord Jesus and if I wanted forgiveness of all my sins. I nodded. I had learned about Jesus in Sunday school. He asked me if I accepted the Heavenly Father into my heart. I nodded again. He put his hand on my head and said something that I no longer remember but I knew it meant that I now had a Heavenly Father.

My body filled with a warm glow and my tears became tears of relief and joy. The empty, hollow, lonely feeling deep inside of me was gone. I almost floated back to my seat, holding onto Mr. Hanson's warm, strong hand. Back in our seats, Mr. Hanson gave me his handkerchief again and I wiped my face.

I loved Mr. Hanson at that moment. I loved Billy Graham. I loved my new Father in Heaven. I wanted to give my brother a hug, but I knew that wouldn't go over very well, so I just smiled at him. He looked at me as if to say, "I don't believe you really went down there."

When we went home that evening, I took with me a Father in Heaven who loved me, who forgave my sins, who would always be with me, who would listen to my problems, and who would protect me. I tucked that secret deep into my heart and carried that glow with me.

Lee's answer to Mom's question about the rally was a quick, "It was okay." When she asked me how I liked it, I hesitated for a moment. How could I tell her about my Father in Heaven? I had asked her once after I started going to Sunday school if she knew about Jesus.

"Of course I do," she said with a disgusted expression. "My grandpa was a preacher. He traveled all over the country preaching at different churches, conducting weddings and funerals and baptizing babies, for all the good it did him. He lay in bed sick for months and died as poor as a church mouse."

No, I didn't think Mom would understand my wonderful new feeling. I didn't want her to ruin my exhilaration by telling me something negative, so I said, "We sang lots of nice songs and Billy Graham preached about the Heavenly Father and we came home. It was fun."

How I wished I could have told her all about my experience— asked her questions. But my gift was so precious, so personal. I couldn't risk having it ruined.

But who could I tell? With whom could I share this wonderful feeling? Who cares?

I couldn't think of anyone except Mr. and Mrs. Hanson, but before the time was right to discuss it, our house burned.

CHAPTER SIX
COMFORT

Mr. and Mrs. Hanson came to pick us up for church again the Sunday after our house burned. Later Mr. Hanson told us he had blinked several times as he approached the driveway. He couldn't believe what he saw. The house was gone!

He drove into the yard and saw only black charred remains of what had been our home. A brick chimney fallen down. Blackened appliances and bed frames. Dirty, trampled snow surrounding the area. A quiet so loud it filled the air.

"We got out of the car and walked cautiously to the house. We didn't know how long ago the house had burned," he said later. "We were afraid of what we might see. We got back into the car and prayed to God that you had all survived."

After a few days of staying with relatives, Dad borrowed money to rent another old farmhouse. Mom set up housekeeping with furniture, bedding, and kitchen utensils our relatives and friends donated to us.

I had asked my Father in Heaven why He let our house burn down. "You're supposed to protect me," I told Him. I didn't get an answer, but I decided that He had been protecting us by not letting the fire start until morning when we were all downstairs. None of us had been hurt. And he protected Mom and Dad as I had asked him. But many other questions still remained on my mind.

The Hansons learned where we were living and came to express their sympathy. Mom made coffee and apologized for not having something to serve with it. Dad was gone, and Mom and Mr. and Mrs. Hanson didn't seem to know what to say to each other. Sandra sat on the stairs with Lee and me in silence. Even Lee kept his eyes downcast and was at a loss for words. What could we say? We were dressed in cast-off clothes that didn't fit. We didn't have a sofa or enough chairs to offer all our guests a seat. We had no food to serve. We felt as pitiful as we looked.

I wanted to ask Mr. Hanson what my Father in Heaven looked like. What was his name? Is He Jesus? Is that who my Heavenly Father is? But I couldn't ask him in front of Mom. They didn't stay long. Mr. Hanson prayed with us and they left. I cried because I knew I'd never see them again. And I didn't. We moved again shortly after that.

Several families brought us used clothing. Before the fire, when someone gave us clothes that didn't fit, Mom altered them. Or else she cut up the garments and used the fabric to make something else. If it was not possible to use the fabric for clothing, she cut it into strips and crocheted rugs. Nothing went to waste in our house. Mom's motto was: Use it up, wear it out, make it do, or do without. But now, since we had nothing else to wear, and no time to make alterations, we wore the clothes as they were, whether they fit or not.

We didn't own much before the fire, but I hadn't felt our poverty. Now I stood in someone else's too-large dress, in a colorless, bare-windowed house, looking at a paint-spattered table, mismatched chairs, worn towels, and a spatula with a broken handle. We had become paupers. Perhaps we didn't deserve better. I could hardly breathe with the heaviness in my chest. I was helpless to make anything better. I didn't know what *would* make things better. I could only cry out silently, "Father in Heaven, Father in Heaven, Father in Heaven."

The next day, a former neighbor came with a gift I have never forgotten. She handed my mother a set of brand new, beautifully hand-embroidered pillowcases. The sight of the pure white cotton cases, folded to display the bright hand-stitched pink, blue, yellow, and green floral design, made me gasp. *Does she mean for us to keep such a beautiful gift?* Everything else around us was old, tattered, and dingy. If we were good enough to receive that gorgeous gift, maybe we *did* deserve beautiful things. Maybe we *were* okay after all. My mother's smile—something I hadn't seen in a while—told me that Mom also felt comforted and validated.

I lifted my chin and calm washed over me. New strength and energy surged through my body. *We will be okay again. Mom can make us new clothes. Life will go on.*

The sun shone though the front windows. I crossed the empty room and sat on the floor, my smiling face lifted to the warm, yellow rays. Irene came and sat in my lap and I put my arms around her in a tight hug. Her giggle made things feel normal.

Our neighbor's generosity was an answer to my fervent cry to my Father in Heaven. I hadn't even known how to pray. But my Father in Heaven heard my cry, knew my need, and gave me more than I knew to ask for. He was there. He loved me, He listened to me, He protected me, and He comforted me. That was only one of many times in my childhood—in my life—that my Father in Heaven kept the promise that Billy Graham told me that day so very long ago.

CHAPTER SEVEN

MOM'S DIFFICULT LIFE

We endured a meager existence for a few weeks in that drafty old house Dad rented after our house fire. Then we moved to a different house. That house was set on the inside curve of a dirt road far out in the country near St. Cloud. Lee and I boarded a big, yellow school bus every morning, leaving our dog, Snowball, standing at the mailbox looking as if he wanted to come with us. At the end of each day I felt dark gloom surround me as our school bus neared that curve in the road. Even Snowball's greeting, wagging his tail at the mailbox, failed to lift the heavy feeling that overcame me each day at that time.

Dad found work at a sales barn and stayed with his Uncle Mib during the week. On Friday night Dad hitchhiked and walked home carrying a gunnysack of groceries over his shoulder. Mom and Dad rolled their own cigarettes with cigarette papers and a red can of Velvet tobacco.

After a few weeks Dad went to Minneapolis on the bus and found work in a brickyard. Once again, he only came home on weekends. He rented a room from Mrs. Lapinski on Fremont Avenue in North Minneapolis during the week.

I don't believe my loneliness and depression that winter came from missing my father, but rather from taking on my mother's sadness and desperation as she tried to make a home out of nothing for her family.

Lee helped out by shooting pheasants and snaring rabbits. Mom cooked them and we thought we were eating "high on the hog," as Dad would say.

One day a neighbor lady who was at school invited Lee and me to go to a movie with her and her family on Saturday. "Ask your mother for permission," she said. I wanted to go to the movie, but I knew it cost money. I didn't want to make Mom feel bad so I didn't ask. Kindness had turned me into a coward.

Early Saturday afternoon, the neighbor lady and her children arrived to pick us up for the movie. Mom knew nothing about it. It turned out it was a free movie. Mom said we could have gone if she had known ahead of time. But since we weren't ready, we couldn't go.

My heart hurt because we had missed the movie, but it hurt more because Lee was angry with me. Lee really wanted to have gone to that movie. I couldn't stand it when Lee was mad at me. I couldn't stand it when Mom was disappointed with me, either, but that seldom happened. I was Mom's "good girl."

I remember that movie incident well because it happened the same Saturday that Lee got his finger stuck in an old, dirty pop bottle he had found. Dad had to break the bottle to free Lee's finger. Mom scolded Lee because they could have sold that bottle for three cents. Lee was already chafing from the morning scolding, and then he lost out on a movie in the afternoon. Not a good day for him.

Looking back, I think few days were good for Mom. Even before she married Dad, she had a difficult life. She grew up on a farm near Menahga, Minnesota, where her father tried to eke out a living for his family of ten children farming rocky, sandy soil. Grandpa Pajari was a willing worker, but he spent most of his income on alcohol, leaving his family struggling to make ends meet.

Then Grandpa slipped on a patch of ice while cutting firewood and the circular saw cut off his left arm. It was a wonder that he lived. After he recovered, he went to Minneapolis to buy a prosthesis, but it was too expensive. He carefully studied how they were made and came home and made his own, an arm that attached by straps across his shoulder, with a sharp steel hook for a hand.

By that time some of his six sons were able to carry on the farming, but Grandpa didn't sit around whining. He first tried selling men's suit fabrics, but he discovered he wasn't a good salesman, so he gave that up and applied for manual labor jobs working on road crews or in lumber camps. When he applied for jobs, he tucked his left shirtsleeve into the front of his bib overalls to camouflage his missing arm. Then, after he was hired, he showed up for work wearing the metal hook. He worked on highway construction, cleared trees, and worked any job he could find. People said he could work as well as any man with two hands.

Grandpa even built a garage for himself. He cut down the trees, hauled them to a lumberyard to be cut into boards, and then built the garage by himself. He held the head of a hammer sideways in his one hand and put the nail between his fingers. He whacked the nail end into the lumber hard enough so it would stay. Then he flipped the hammer in his hand and pounded in the nail. He was intelligent and hard working.

When Mom was seven years old she became ill during a spinal meningitis epidemic. Her younger brother, Fred, had died a few weeks earlier of that same disease. Mom was not only grieving Fred's death, but also saddened because Fred never got the red snowsuit pictured in the Sears and Roebuck catalog that he wanted so badly.

When the illness hit Mom, it didn't take long before she too collapsed from the disease. Later Mom said she followed a bright light to heaven, and her brother Fred met her there. He was wearing a red snowsuit. She was totally delighted to see her brother, but he told her it wasn't her time yet and she had to go back. Mom protested, but Fred insisted that she go back.

In the meantime, Mom's parents had put a sheet over her face and put her in a cold room. Her father went to New York Mills to buy long white stockings and a small coffin for her burial. Mom's brother, Chester, went into the cold bedroom, pulled the sheet back from her face, and looked at her. He saw her eyelid move. "She's alive," he yelled to his mother as he ran from the room. And, indeed, she was alive again.

Every time Mom told me that story, she smiled and said, "I was so happy to see that Fred got his little red snowsuit after all."

Mom wasn't one to talk about God. She never attended church. But she had absolutely no fear of dying because she said, "I died once and it was wonderful. I'll go back there anytime God wants to take me." Ironically, Mom was born on December 7, a date that later became a date in infamy. She died on September 11, also a date that two years later became another date in infamy. Between those two terrible dates, she lived a difficult life of much unhappiness.

School was challenging for Mom at first because she only spoke the Finnish language, and her teacher punished children who didn't speak English in school. She did learn English, but she attended school only through eighth grade.

When Mom was fourteen, her parents couldn't afford to send her to high school because she would have to buy books and clothes and pay rent to stay in town. So Mom wanted to go to Minneapolis to work. Grandpa drove her to Menahga in a horse and buggy, told her to hitch a ride with a truck driver going to Minneapolis, and left her at a gas station. She sat at the station for three days waiting for a truck driver, but none came. Each evening she walked to her cousin Eleanor's house, in shoes full of holes, and stayed overnight. After the third day, Eleanor loaned Mom three dollars to take the bus to the city.

Mom stayed with her older sister, Jennie, when she first arrived in Minneapolis. She found a job as a maid in a private residence earning three dollars a week. She worked six and a half days a week with Sunday afternoons off. When she got her first paycheck, she sent the whole three dollars to Eleanor to repay what she had borrowed. When she received her second paycheck she spent $2.98 for a pair of new shoes.

Mom's boss asked Mom to spend a week at the lake with her family. There, the woman's nephew did mean things and blamed them on Mom. They went out into the middle of the lake and the nephew tried to push Mom out of the boat. When Mom reported it, the boy said Mom tried to push him out. They scolded Mom.

Back in the city Mom packed her bag and asked for the wages owed her. Her boss begged her to stay, offering her a raise, and said she would no longer have to do laundry. Mom left anyway, saying, "You didn't believe me, so I can't work for you any longer."

Mom got another job working as a maid for a Jewish family, but this time Mom insisted on having Sundays off. When they made a big meal on Sunday and brought Mom only a chicken wing, she said, "It's against my religion to eat the wing." They brought her a nice breast. Another time when they brought her sewing to do on Sunday, her day off, she said it was against her religion to sew on Sunday. It worked again.

The woman Mom worked for often said, "Just junk it," when Mom asked her what to do with various things she found laying around the house. One day Mom saw something unusual-looking in the refrigerator and asked the woman what it was. "Junk it," she told Mom. So Mom emptied the bowl of stuff into the garbage.

Later that evening the woman said, "Where is the bowl of dessert that was in the refrigerator?"

Mom said, "I asked you what it was and you said 'junk it,' so I threw it away." It was a boxed dessert mix called Junket. Mom didn't get paid that week.

When Mom was eighteen, she moved to Memphis, Tennessee, with a girlfriend. She played the guitar and had hopes of becoming a singer. She became a waitress instead. It was there that she met a handsome young man named Robert Duncan, who was also from Minnesota. He worked at building an underground sewer system, earning $25.00 a week. That was a good income. He told Mom she had the prettiest silver-blonde hair he had ever seen.

Dad didn't have a car, so they either walked or took the bus to the movies or wherever they wanted to go. Not long after Mom turned nineteen, they were married. Shortly thereafter, they returned to Minnesota. For Dad it was to a life of hard work, anger, and inadequacies. For Mom it was to a life of pregnancies and poverty.

I didn't learn that Mom had once played the guitar until long after I was married. I never saw a guitar or heard my mother sing. No lullabies. No singing along with the radio. When I tried to get Mom to tell me about happy times in her life, she always said, "Oh, I can't remember."

I wonder who took the music from Mom's soul. Was it Dad? Or was it the fear of life that most of Mom's siblings also lived with? My uncle once told me that their mother frightened them about things. Mom was terribly scared of thunderstorms. Had she also been afraid of trying to make her dream come true? Had someone told her she couldn't sing, and she decided to never sing again? Mom wouldn't answer questions about it.

I didn't like my mother's negative philosophy about things. As a young girl, I often told myself that I would not be like my mother when I grew up. Yet, my gloomy mood matched my mother's that winter and seemed to carry over into my school days.

CHAPTER EIGHT

MY SIN

Riding a school bus and attending school in town was a new experience for me, having attended only country schools since first grade. At this school, where I was still in fourth grade, students were allowed to go to a little mom-and-pop grocery store across the street to buy candy after we ate our lunches. I never went to the store because I never had money. But one day, when another girl asked me to go to the store with her, I agreed.

We stood waiting for the flag patrol to allow us to cross the street—lots of rowdy boys shoving each other, and little girls holding hands—all going to the store for candy. I shuffled my feet through the slippery snow and listened to the swishing sound of corduroy pants rubbing between the thighs of a chubby boy walking in front of us.

The candy counter behind a glass front, just inside the door, was a poor kid's fantasy. Baby Ruth and Snickers bars, chocolate Milk Duds, sticky taffy, penny candy, little cellophane strips of colorful gumballs, shiny cinnamon Red Hots, Lifesavers, and candy of every color and shape stared at me. On top of the counter, just at eye level, was more candy. Long strips of black licorice, shiny brown root beer barrels, and big, fat, all-day suckers with red and green stripes winding around them like barbershop poles.

The sweet smells made my mouth water. I wanted some candy, but I had no money. I wondered if anyone would see me if I took just one piece of licorice. I looked around. No one was watching. I looked at the licorice again, but my eyes moved over to the big, fat suckers. *A sucker would last longer.* Before I could reason with myself I was out the door with my stolen goods, my heart pounding, my hand tightly gripping a sucker. I didn't even wait for my friend, but ran back to school by myself.

I sat beneath a tree inside the schoolyard and licked the sucker. It was sweet and sticky. I took another lick, and another, and another. It smelled like cinnamon. After the heavenly taste of the fist few licks, a terrible guilt took away my enjoyment.

By now most of the kids had returned from the store and I knew the bell would ring soon. My sucker was still so big. I licked it faster but it wasn't getting any smaller. I tried to bite into it but it was too hard, so I just kept licking faster and faster. My tongue was getting sore.

The bell rang but I didn't know what to do with my sucker. I couldn't go into the schoolroom with the evidence of my crime, so I started to cry.

I sat there under the tree crying and licking that sucker as fast as I could. The faster I licked, the harder I cried. That's when my teacher came out and found me. She asked me what was wrong, but I couldn't answer. I nodded when she finally asked me if I was sick. She helped me up and took me to the nurse's office.

The nurse took my sucker and wrapped it in some paper and said I could have it back when I left. I spent the entire afternoon on the cot in the nurse's office. My stomach hurt. My head hurt. My heart hurt. I had stolen something. That was a sin. I was afraid that my Father in Heaven was angry with me. Maybe he didn't love me anymore.

When we got on the school bus, I gave my sucker to Lee and told him that my girlfriend bought it for me. Now I had added lying to my sins.

At home, I crawled into bed and refused to talk to anyone or to get up for supper. I felt so awful. But as I lay there, I remembered that Billy Graham had said that my Father in Heaven would forgive my sins and make me pure again. "I'm so sorry, Father in Heaven," I cried. "I'm sorry. Will you forgive me and make me pure again, please? I'm sorry. I won't ever steal anything again."

After a while I went to sleep. I never told anyone what I did that day, and I've kept my promise. I never stole anything again. Ever.

CHAPTER NINE

SUMMER AND BLUEBERRIES

That June, I turned ten. When school was out for the summer, my mother asked someone to take us to Mrs. Lapinski's in Minneapolis.

Had Mom reached a breaking point and was just unable to continue living out in the country with no adult companionship all week? Or did she suspect that Dad was being unfaithful while he lived away from home? Dad was extremely handsome, with black wavy hair, dark eyes, and a great smile.

But, whatever the reason, we showed up unannounced that day and sat in Dad's small room, trying to be quiet so we wouldn't disturb Mrs. Lapinski. All except for Judie, that is. Somehow she managed to escape Mom's watchful eye, and mine as well, and we found her standing in the middle of the street, arms spread wide, laughing and singing: "Ha, ha, no cars can run over me-eee." I don't know who cried harder as Mom spanked Judie—Judie because she was being spanked, Mom because she had been certain her little daughter was about to be hit by a car on busy Fremont Avenue before she could reach her, or me because Mom and Judie were crying.

I have no memory of Dad's reaction when he found us all waiting for him when he got home. He must have been surprised. Was he angry? Did Mom and Dad argue? Were ultimatums given? I don't remember.

We stayed about a week, and then Dad moved us to a rented farmhouse just outside of Pease, Minnesota. The owner of the house also owned a sales barn, and Dad got a job working there with his cousin, Howard Duncan.

That was the best summer of my childhood. We lived close enough to Dad's cousin Howard that we visited a lot back and forth with my many second cousins. I learned to ride a bicycle up and down their long driveway. How I enjoyed that! It was probably the first indication of my love for travel. I just wanted to ride down their driveway, down the roadway, and on and on to wherever it would take me. We didn't have a bicycle, but they were generous and let me ride theirs a lot when we went to visit them.

Unlike our family, Howard's children were musical, and I derived such pleasure listening to Janet and Jean Ann harmonizing together as they sang song after song. Janet also played the guitar and yodeled. I joined in to sing "Mockingbird Hill" and many other country classics of that era.

Mom and Mabel, Howard's wife, sat at the table, drank coffee, and visited. My mother was happy during that time in her life. She enjoyed her friendship with Mabel, and our families spent many hours together that year.

Another fun thing we enjoyed that summer was visiting with Dad's uncle, Ray Ingram, and his family. I never knew how to react to the kids in that family. They told dirty jokes that I didn't understand and they swore like sailors. I just took it all in and watched my brother grin. Sometimes I later asked Lee to explain a joke to me. He just grinned and said, "You wouldn't understand," or "You're too young to know that."

Uncle Ray had an old, rusty pickup, and he frequently took all us kids to an outdoor movie. I've lost count of how many kids there were because the count included his kids, and his sister's kids, and his grandkids, and us. Aunt Belle threw a bunch of blankets in the bed of the truck and we all covered up with them while we traveled down the dusty, gravel roads to town.

One of the older boys kissed me under the blanket in the dark. I was only about 10, and he was probably in high school, but he didn't care, and neither did I. That was my first experience being kissed by a boy, and it was quite exciting. No one else saw us and he didn't touch me inappropriately in any other way, so I felt safe. He kissed me several times, and I didn't resist. He kissed me many times on the way home again. He was one of Uncle Ray's sister's children and was only there for that one movie. I was sorry he wasn't there for the other movies.

The movies we saw that summer were mostly Ma and Pa Kettle movies. I couldn't help but make the comparison with our own pickup full of ragtag kids, and I thought we weren't too far removed from those hillbillies.

So why did we move again that fall? Did Dad get angry with his boss? Was he fired? Or did his *gypsy* blood nudge him on to greener pastures again? Dad moved us to a third floor apartment in what used to be the old Ransford Hotel in Brainerd until he could come back for us. Then he went to Montana where my uncle Jack had gotten him a job at the same logging camp where Uncle Jack worked.

Lee, Donna, Judie, and I started school in Brainerd that fall. Judie was in first grade. Lee was eleven and a half. He was strong and tough. Somehow he got a job evenings and weekends setting pins at a bowling alley next door. He earned ten cents a line. Back then automatic pinsetters didn't exist. The people hired to set pins stood behind the pins with their feet on raised boxes. After the bowling ball hit the pins, it was the pinsetter's job to jump down and reset the pins and then jump back up out of harm's way again.

I stood at our third-floor window and looked out at the cascading lights of the movie theater that sat kitty-corner across the street and below our apartment. I worried about Lee. *What if one of those pins hits him?* It was possible. Sometimes those pins jumped up pretty high with a lot of force.

I wondered if my Father in Heaven would protect my brother liked he protected me. If he was my Father in Heaven, could he be my brother's Father in Heaven too? Lee hadn't gone down to the front to have Billy Graham give him a Father in Heaven. I wished I could ask someone, but I didn't know whom to ask. Mom wouldn't know. On the slim chance that it would work, I asked my Father in Heaven to protect Lee from getting hurt. It seemed to work.

"Blueberries again?" Lee asked one day when we came home from school for lunch. We had been eating Mom's home-canned blueberry sauce and bread and butter three times a day in that Brainerd apartment. Last summer Mom had gone blueberry picking several times a week for about a month. Often Lee had gone with her while I watched the girls. Sometimes she went with my aunt.

"Daddy's going to send us some money pretty soon," Mom said in response to Lee's question. "Then we can buy something else. This is all we have for now."

Although she watched the mail eagerly, week after week, the money Mom was expecting didn't come. At mealtime Mom opened yet another quart jar of blueberry sauce. We no longer had bread and butter to go with it. At each meal Mom said, "What would we have done now if the blueberry crop wasn't so good last summer?"

I knew that my Father in Heaven had made the crop good so we would have food now. After all, Billy Graham said He would protect me. I silently said, "Thank you" to my Father in Heaven, but I didn't tell Mom why we had so many blueberries. She probably wouldn't believe me. After all, even being a preacher hadn't made a difference in her grandpa's life. But I truly believed that the abundant blueberry crop was for my benefit. My faith was strong.

CHAPTER TEN
LIKE A THIEF IN THE NIGHT

Then, without warning, Dad came home in the middle of the night. Mom awakened us five children and told us to be very quiet. "We're leaving tonight," she whispered. "Daddy's taking us to Montana with him. Get dressed quickly. Be very quiet."

Dad loaded Mom's sewing machine and a few boxes of belongings into a small trailer hitched to the car while we got dressed and got into the back seat. "Why aren't we taking our beds?" I asked as Dad drove quietly away into the darkness of the night.

"We don't have room to take everything," Mom said from the front seat where she held Irene.

"But where will we sleep if we don't have our beds? And where will we eat if we don't have our table?" Clearly I didn't understand this move at all.

Mom turned in her seat to look at me. "Honey, we don't have money to pay the rent, so we left those things there for our landlord to sell to pay for the rent. We'll be okay. Daddy says everything we need is already in our new house." Mom sniffled as if she was crying.

I hung tightly on to my Father in Heaven because I was afraid of a future without our furniture and our things, and I could tell Mom was upset about it too. Many miles down the road I said, "My pearl purse! Where's my pearl purse?"

"I'm sorry, honey," Mom said, "I didn't think about your purse."

I sobbed. My Aunt Alice had given me that clutch bag covered in tiny pearls. "For when you grow up and go to dances," she had told me. I had frequently opened the box, unwrapped the pink tissue paper, took out the purse, and dreamed of the day I would be old enough to wear makeup and a fancy dress and go to dances. Now my purse was gone forever. Why didn't I think about my purse when Mom said we were leaving? How could Mom forget my favorite thing in the whole world? Why did Dad have to take us to Montana anyway? *Father in Heaven, why did you let us forget my purse?* I cried until Lee started calling me a crybaby and our argument replaced my tears. I stayed angry with my Heavenly Father for a long time.

The road trip to the logging camp near White Sulphur Springs, Montana, was long and arduous. We had no way for us four oldest children to distance ourselves from each other in the back seat. While Judie often leaned on me to sleep, it was difficult for me to get comfortable enough to doze. Much of the time my stomach also hurt with hunger. The cities were far apart. When we came to a town around mealtime, Dad always found a grocery store and stopped. He went into the store while the rest of us stood outside to stretch our legs. Then he came back with a loaf of white Wonder bread, a package of sliced bologna, and a six-pack of Orange Crush soda pop. We eagerly piled back into the car.

Dad opened the first pop bottle and handed it back to Lee. The "pop-fizz" had me salivating before my turn came, as Dad gave each of us four children in the back seat our own bottle of cold, thirst-quenching pop. Mom shared hers with Irene in the front seat.

As Dad drove off, Mom put a slice of bologna between two slices of soft, delicious Wonder bread and handed the sandwich back to each of us in turn. It was heaven! This was our mealtime routine during that trip.

As an adult, just the smell of bologna brings back memories of being in the back seat of that car watching the badlands of North Dakota and the mountains of Montana passing by our windows. That bologna sandwich and bottle of Orange Crush was a taste treat that, to this day, I sometimes crave.

Dad was driving a 1935 Plymouth, pulling a homemade rough-cut pine trailer, traveling about thirty miles per hour on that trip to Montana. When we got to Glendive, North Dakota, the rods in the car started knocking fiercely. Dad didn't have the money to fix the car.

He called his boss for an advance on his wages and we waited all day for the car to be repaired and the money to be wired to us. We were tired, bored, and hungry. When we got the money we all went into a restaurant—the first time I had ever eaten in a restaurant.

Food had never tasted so good to me! I silently thanked my Heavenly Father for the money and for the good food.

CHAPTER ELEVEN

TARPAPER SHACK

When we got to the logging camp near Forest Green in Montana, I was shocked to see our new house. It was a one-room tarpaper shack with no electricity or running water. The furnishings were a rough-cut picnic table, two long benches, and a few army cots. A pot-bellied wood stove sat right in the middle of the room. A two-burner kerosene stove for cooking and a hole in the ground behind our shack for refrigeration rounded out our kitchen needs. I was even angrier with my Father in Heaven now. How could He do this to me?

It took a long time for the fire in the stove to heat the shack. I helped Mom put pillows and blankets on the narrow army cots lined up against the outside walls—walls that consisted of bare studs covering rough lumber with tarpaper tacked on the outside of that. The floors were also rough lumber; the table and benches were rough lumber. The windows were small. The shack was dark. I hated it!

Outside, every direction I looked, mountains seemed to dwarf us, situated in a valley as we were. Three other tarpaper shacks sat in our little valley community called "The Family Camp," with enough distance from each other to provide privacy. We got water from a spring a couple hundred feet from our shack. I knew from our drive getting there that we were way out in the middle of nowhere—many miles from any town.

Before we had time to halfway settle in, my mother's sister, Lila, who lived in the farthest shack, came over with a meal to welcome us to Montana. Her three sons came along as well— Dwight, Gerald, and Arlan—Arlan being no more than a toddler at the time. As happy as I was to see my aunt and my cousins, can you imagine how happy my mother had to be to see another female adult in that forlorn place? My mother's brother, Bill, and his wife, Betty, lived in another of the shacks, and Billy and Mary Williams, who had one young boy, lived in the only other shack in that little family camp.

It was a long, cold, winter. We had about five feet of snow on the ground and Dad worked in the woods all day, cutting trees with a chainsaw. First he had to scoop snow to get to the trunk of the tree. After he had the tree cut and ready to fall, he threw his chainsaw up out of the hole he was working in and quickly grabbed the tree to catch a ride up and out of the hole. Sometimes he was six feet down. Not easy work.

While the men worked in the snow, the boys played in it. Dwight and Lee lay together on a hand-steered sled and slid down a hill that was so long and steep that any little bump would knock the wind out of them.

Life in the logging camp had a whole different feel than what I was used to in Minnesota. Here, when we needed food, the men got together at night and shined deer. It was illegal, but they didn't have time to hunt during the day because they worked until dark. Besides, it wasn't for sport—it was to feed their families. What could be wrong about that, they told each other.

They hung the deer from a tree for a few days and then brought it onto the rough kitchen table and cut it up. Then Mom cleaned the pieces well, cut off all the fat, and canned the venison in quart jars.

She did all that on a two-burner kerosene stove. Just remembering how delicious that venison tasted still makes my mouth water. I have never tasted meat that good since then.

Given the distance from town, and the fact that my mother never learned to drive a car, the women in the camp all went together on shopping trips. There was no room for children.

School was another new experience. My Aunt Lila drove Dwight, Lee, Donna, Judie, and me a mile to the school bus stop, and we rode for twenty miles to school at White Sulphur Springs. As the new fifth grade girl, I was immediately popular. Jack Ranta and Wesley Skerrit fought each other for my attention. I didn't understand why. I was pale faced with dishwater blonde hair and I wasn't pretty—not like one of the older girls on the school bus whom I admired so much. She had long black hair and long pink fingernails, and she wore soft sweaters. She had a habit of massaging the sides of her nail beds. Of course, I decided that was what made them grow so long and beautiful. So I began massaging the sides of my nails as well. It never helped.

During that year, my wardrobe consisted of two pairs of blue denim jeans, one light yellow cotton blouse, and one yellow knit shirt with a brown stripe across my chest. Since I only had two shirts, it would have been nice if they had, at least, been different colors. At the end of the year I was voted "The Girl with the Best Posture," so I guess people noticed something other than my limited wardrobe.

I had no right to complain about my clothes with what my mother went through. On Wednesdays, when we got home from school, as usual, we changed into our *everyday* clothes, meaning the only other pair of jeans and shirts we had. Mom laid out those *school* clothes on the rough table and spot-washed them with a wet brush so we could manage to look clean until Saturday. Some time during a weekday she washed our *everyday* clothes and had them dry by the time we got home from school. On Saturday, she scrubbed our school clothes. All the laundry for her family of seven was done on a scrub board in a gray, galvanized washtub. No washing machines there, nor electricity with which to operate them.

Dad worked hard, doing what he had to do to support his family. Mom worked just as hard, or harder, to do what was necessary to care for us as well. I didn't fully appreciate them, and all they did for us, at the time. Why do we learn after it is too late? I wonder what I still haven't learned.

CHAPTER TWELVE

MONTANA

In Montana, once again I was relegated to "mother's helper" with no girl my own age to play with. Dwight wasn't much younger than I, but he paired up with my brother, of course, leaving me out, except when they needed more hands for a game such as Annie-I-Over that we sometimes played during long summer evenings.

While my brother and Dwight curled themselves up in rubber tires and rolled down the mountainside, hunted squirrels with slingshots, and practiced twirling a lasso, I watched my three little sisters. But now I had access to magazines. My Aunt Betty bought romance magazines that she let me read. I gobbled them up in no time at all and asked for another. Living in isolation as we did, it was often weeks before she had another magazine for me. Again, I was often lonely.

Sometimes, when my chest hurt from loneliness, I thought about my Father in Heaven. Thinking about Him made me feel warm and cozy, like I was Daddy's Little Girl. I felt like He had His arms around me, holding me close, telling me He loved me, and that I was special. I relied on Him for comfort over and over.

That summer I also embroidered my first project—a dresser scarf. It was from a stamped embroidery kit that my Aunt Alice had given me for my birthday. Butterflies of many colors graced the long piece of fabric. When I finished it, I spread it atop an upturned peach crate that I had placed between Irene's and my cot. It gave the room an elegance that it otherwise lacked—as nothing else of beauty could be seen in the whole shack.

I spent most of that following summer outdoors watching my little sisters so they didn't get into trouble. That meant to not let them get too far away from the shack. Wild animals—bears, cougars, bobcats, and lynx—were spotted frequently in the area. One day Billie Williams came back to camp with a bobcat he had shot. Not long afterward a forest ranger came and said a mountain lion was spotted in the area. He told Mom to keep the kids indoors for a few days.

Mom and Lila and Betty visited each other frequently. Each was busy keeping their family's needs met, but we visited back and forth. Arlan was often a naughty boy, and Aunt Lila spanked him. He grabbed onto Aunt Lila's leg and cried and cried, even while she walked around the room. I thought that was such a foolish thing to do. If Mom gave me a spanking, I wouldn't want to talk to her for a long time. I sure wouldn't want to hang on to her. But then, how would I know? Mom had never spanked me.

One day Mom wrote this song:

Life in the West
By Merle Duncan

We finally came to Montana,
But no use wearing a bandana,
'Cause nobody sees us in this brush.
All there's here is mud and slush.
Around us mountains are like a wall,
And hundreds of trees, so huge and tall.
So what's the use for fancy duds out here?

The shacks are black and some quite small.
On the inside cardboard covers the wall,
With iron cots to sleep in at night.
But warm we stay, you doggone right.
With rough-sawed shelves and benches and tables
And nowhere in miles an electric cable.
So what's the use to work too late at night?

The theaters are far and the roads are rough.
Hills and curves and all that stuff.
Through the canyon and over the pass
We bounce along like an old jackass.
Dust so thick it stings your nose,
And oh! So much dust settles on the clothes.
So what's the use to go on any sprees?

Don't dare to eat much chocolate candy,
'Cause the doctors are not handy.
But as you can see by this song,
We must all be brave and strong.
Every day the children ride
For miles to learn to read and write.
So what's the use to fret and worry and mope?

Such is life, but it's all fun
The trees, the mountains, and the sun.
All beautiful, I should say,
If we could always live this way.
Less work when all the rooms combine
Not even any stairs to climb.
But for pleasure, there is never any time.

I wasn't aware of that song until I was an adult and Mom shared it with me one day. "It was just something to do besides work," she said as she showed me the aged, yellowed tablet paper she had written it on. When I asked her to tell me more about that time in Montana, she just shrugged. "It was a long time ago," she said. She wouldn't comment further. I think she didn't want to remember.

CHAPTER THIRTEEN

SCARED STIFF

We had a few harrowing experiences while we were at that logging camp. Because my toes had such severe frostbite when our house burned, I always sat in the front seat of the school bus behind the driver where the heat was the warmest. One day when our school bus was bringing us home from school, a pulp truck met us around the curve of a mountain road with an uneven load. The protruding log went through the window where I sat and hit my head.

The doctor sent me home with instructions to my parents to not let me go to sleep for a certain number of hours. So there I was, so sleepy that I couldn't keep my eyes open, and Mom telling me to keep sweeping the floor to stay awake. I hated sweeping that rough wood floor at any time, because it was difficult to get it clean. Now I swept and swept and cried with exhaustion until I couldn't even see what I was doing.

I didn't get better, and I ended up in the hospital at Townsend with a brain concussion. Townsend is seventy miles from where we lived. The doctor kept me there for a month.

Lee had the next health crisis. One day he told Mom, "I swallowed a nail."

"What do you mean, you swallowed a nail?" Mom asked.

"I was playing with it while I was lying on my back and all of a sudden it fell into my mouth and I swallowed it."

"How big was it?

"It was an eight-penny nail."

"Oh, good gracious! That's a huge nail! We've got to get you to a doctor." Of course Mom didn't drive and Dad was at work. "Connie, run to Lila's and tell her to come quick."

My Aunt Lila drove to the logging site and got Dad. Dad then drove Mom and Lee to the closest doctor in Townsend. For some reason that doctor sent them to the Great Falls Hospital—120 miles away. Their x-ray showed a large nail in Lee's intestine. "It should pass with no problems," the doctor said. "If he has any pain, bring him back. Watch his stool. It should pass within three days." Mom examined every stool Lee had, and the third day the nail appeared. I think Lee still has that nail.

Another fright for my mother was when Irene, who was only about five at the time, decided to play at driving Dad's car that was parked on an incline. She got into the car and put it in neutral, and the car rolled down the incline. She was too small to see it, but she remembered that a tree grew in the path of the car so she turned the wheel sharply and kept driving in circles. Just as the rest of us noticed what was happening, Uncle Jack was already running to her rescue. He jumped into the car and got it stopped. Mom had been almost hysterical with fear, but Irene was laughing and wanted to do it again.

Sightings of bobcat and lynx near the camp put more fear into Mom. Then a bear began roaming our camp at night, sniffing around the wooden covers of the deep holes that protected our perishable foods. The men in camp took turns staying up at night with rifles ready to shoot the worrisome bear, but night after night, the bear eluded them.

Then came the night that I awoke with the sound of a bear rubbing its nose against the tarpaper just behind my head, breathing heavily, snorting, sniffing my smell.

I wanted to yell for my dad, who slept only on the other side of the hanging bedspread wall a few feet from me, but my throat wouldn't work. I couldn't make a noise. I was paralyzed with fear.

Soon the bear stood on two legs and began to rub his nose against the window just above my head. I thought I would die of fright. *Could the bear reach through the window and grab me?* "Heavenly Father, Heavenly Father," I silently implored. Eventually the bear moved on and I was able to put enough energy into my legs to get me to Dad's bedside where I told him, in a quaking voice, that the bear had been behind me. *Scared stiff. Paralyzed by fear.* Those are terms that I learned the meaning of that night.

Another night a few weeks later, Dad awoke to hear a bear digging around in the yard where we had a food hole, covered with plywood. Dad had put a large rock on the plywood so animals couldn't get to it. Soon the bear was at our door, snorting and clawing. By then, we were all awake. The bear was pounding so hard on the door that the dishes started falling off the kitchen shelf. Mom shoved us girls under their bed and pulled some cupboard boxes in front of us.

I peeked out at them from the end of the bed and saw Mom holding a long kitchen knife, Lee had an ax, and Dad had a long gun to his shoulder, ready to shoot the bear the minute it appeared. My sisters were all crying. The pounding stopped and I saw the tips of long, black claws slide into the room from under the door. I screamed, and whispered, *Heavenly Father, Heavenly Father, Heavenly Father.*

Earlier, a ranger had told the men that a rogue grizzly was on the prowl. So Dad had nailed holders on each side of the door and brought in a heavy beam that he put across the door every night as a barricade. Now that added protection was working. After a while the bear gave up his attack and moved away. *Thank you, Heavenly Father.*

None of us at the family camp had telephones, so we couldn't warn the others about the bear in the area until the next day. None of them had heard or seen the bear.

That was the last straw for Mom. School ended in a couple weeks and we all moved back to Minnesota to live with Mom's parents temporarily. Not ideal, for certain, but I imagine Mom thought anything was better than living in Montana in that tarpaper shack, fighting off grizzly bears.

CHAPTER FOURTEEN

GRANDPA

It was 1953 and Dad got a job building the new Highway 71 north of Park Rapids, Minnesota. That summer we lived with my mother's parents—John and Alina Pajari—at their farm, a long drive from Park Rapids. Grandma moved so quietly she was almost invisible, but Grandpa was recognizable, even if you didn't see him, because of the smell of wool clothing, whisky, and Copenhagen snuff. With the exception of his very blue eyes, his color was gray—from his gray hair and beard to his denim bib overalls worn colorless. His skin was rawhide leather, thick, worn, and creased. He spent many hours sitting under a tree, turning a big, round, grindstone with a foot pedal, sharpening tools. He held the sharp end against the wheel with his only hand, the handle tucked tight beneath his right arm.

Grandpa's father was Peter, one of seven Pajari brothers, born in Trondheim, Norway, who had been auctioned to different families after their parents both died. Some took on their new families' names, and some changed the "P" to "B." When they grew up, all seven brothers worked on fishing boats. They eventually all immigrated to the United States and settled in Minnesota. I never knew my great-grandfather Peter or his wife.

Grandpa John laughed and tolerated my little sisters sitting on his lap and putting braids in his beard, but I don't recall a single sentence he ever spoke to me. The old adage that children should be seen but not heard went a step further in that house. I don't think I was even seen most of the time.

However, Grandpa drove into town about once a week. He always brought home a Snickers candy bar for each of us five children. So we waited eagerly for his return from town in his old, black, Model T Ford. We were careful to watch our manners, so we didn't run to the car with our hands out. Instead we sat on the front steps, or generally hung around there, easily accessible to Grandpa when he arrived home.

Grandpa took great pride in his strawberry patch alongside the driveway. "Stay out of the strawberries," he told us. "You'll step on the berries." He spent hours in the sun on his knees, pulling weeds, transplanting runners, and picking berries. He sold them in town for 35 cents a quart. But throughout the whole strawberry season, whenever Grandpa walked into the house with a pail of berries, he invited us to share them.

Mom and Grandma washed and cleaned the berries while we watched them, our mouths more eager by the minute for our first taste. Then we all sat around the big, oak table and ate our bowl of ripe, red strawberries, warm from the sun, smothered in sugar and rich, cold cream scooped from the top of the cream can. It didn't matter what time of day it was—when Grandpa came in with a pail of fresh strawberries, we stopped whatever we were doing and enjoyed that delicious treat.

I still think of Grandpa when I pick strawberries. It is hard, backbreaking work. He must have loved us a lot to see us consume so much of his profit and hard work.

Grandma, Grandpa, Uncle Harvey, Uncle Richard, Uncle Glen, Mom, Dad, and we five children all occupied that house the whole summer when I turned twelve. The house was small. An entryway, just large enough for one person to occupy at a time, led to a door opening into a big kitchen where a long table, covered in oilcloth and flanked by two long benches, took up most of the space. The only other furniture in that main room of the house was an imposing wood cook stove toward the back of the room, a dry sink with a water pump near the door, and a long wooden bench in front of the sunny south window that always held a well-read pile of newspapers written in Finnish. The living room was a combination reading room, radio room, and bedroom. Guests always sat around the kitchen table to drink coffee and visit.

That kitchen table was the hub of the house. In the center of the table sat a kerosene lamp with a wick that frequently needed to be trimmed and a glass globe that needed daily washing. In the evening, when some of us sat around the table reading, Grandpa came and turned the wick way down until we could hardly see to read the words on the page. "Don't waste the kerosene," he always said. We never considered telling him that we needed more light to continue reading. That wouldn't have been polite.

A glass with teaspoons sticking out of it like a bouquet of flowers, and an orange sugar bowl that we didn't recognize at the time as valuable carnival glass, were also permanent fixtures on the table. Instead of sugar granules, the sugar bowl held little square cubes of sugar that were off-limits to us children.

Most people put a couple cubes of sugar in their cup of coffee, but Grandma put a sugar cube in her mouth, poured a little hot coffee, with cream, from her cup into her saucer, and sipped coffee from the saucer through the sugar cube in her mouth. I remember thinking it was because she was Swedish, even though Finnish was their language. That was just one more bit of mystery that surrounded my grandmother.

The wood stove that heated the house in the winter stood in the center of the living room. Mom's single bed was against the wall next to the stove with Dad's single bed across the room. In a house so crowded with people, I suppose that was the best they could hope for. It was only temporary.

Two hard chairs flanked a library table with a radio sitting upon it. That radio was our favorite form of recreation. Uncle Glen and Lee liked to listen to boxing matches, especially when Rocky Marciano was fighting. Lee and I watched the clock, ready to turn on the radio when The Gene Autry, Roy Rogers, or Wild Bill Hickok Show came on. Many times we sat with our ears next to the radio, listening tensely to an exciting part of the show, when Grandpa came into the room, turned off the radio and said, "Don't wear out the batteries." More than once, we left the room, crestfallen.

Grandma's and Grandpa's bedroom was just off the kitchen. The other bedroom on the main floor of that house was just through the living room. It had beds against three of the walls. My three uncles occupied that room.

Donna, Judie, and I slept in the large bed in the attic, and Lee slept in the smaller bed next to it. Mom made a bed on the floor for Irene. I don't remember feeling crowded, and I don't believe that either Grandpa or Grandma made my parents feel unwelcome, but I imagine Mom and Dad felt that for so many people, it was small quarters.

CHAPTER FIFTEEN

GRANDMA

Alina Ruokangas Pajari, my maternal grandmother, couldn't speak English, and I couldn't speak Finnish. So we hadn't spoken to each other those several weeks our family had been staying with them. But I wanted to talk to Grandma. I wanted to know her. I wanted her to know me. I wanted her to like me.

Grandma Alina had come to America as a child on a ship from Finland. She was born in 1891 to Swedish and Finnish parents Gust and Elizabeth (Elsie) Moilanen Ruokangas. Gust was a Lutheran minister who traveled to different churches performing weddings, baptisms, and funerals. His wife Elsie was a midwife who delivered babies wherever she was needed. They had eight children. Alina was one of the oldest, and another child was born on the ship coming to America. The others were born in rural Minnesota, near Menagha, where Indians often walked right into their house. Elsie always gave them whatever they wanted—food, tobacco, or alcohol. Trembling with fear, she cooked and fed them at her table. They always came when she was alone, but they never harmed her or the children.

So my Grandma Alina grew up in modest means with little education. It is told that when she was very young, Grandpa John Pajari walked many miles to court her. They were married in 1908 when Grandma was seventeen years old. They had ten children.

Grandma Alina had a plain face, and she wore brown stockings twisted into knots just above her knees. Of course, you couldn't see the knots until she sat down or if she was bending over, but once I knew they were there, I always envisioned them, even when her flowered housedress and the apron she always wore covered the knots. I couldn't imagine anyone wearing anything that looked so uncomfortable.

Every morning Grandma coiled her hip-length, brown hair into a bun on the top of her head and held it in place with long hairpins. Then in the evening, after she changed into her nightgown and flannel robe, she sat on the bench by the window and pulled the long hairpins from her bun. While I listened to Grandpa's radio, I watched her brush her hair until it shone in the light of the kerosene lamp. Then she braided it into a thick braid for the night.

Grandma spoke softly and walked quietly as if being careful to not awaken a sleeping child or cause a cake in the oven to fall. She was the closest thing to a ghost that I had ever seen, moving about silently as she did. Grandma was the only one allowed to use a chamber pot in her bedroom, while everyone else had to walk the well-worn path to the outhouse, no matter how dark the night. The door creaked, and a tattered Sears and Roebuck catalog did our *cleanup*.

On Saturday nights we all walked the path that ran behind the house to the sauna, taking turns—women and children first—for our Saturday night baths. Grandpa had a hot wood fire in the stove surrounded by big rocks. When the rocks were hot enough, he began dipping water from a bucket and pouring it onto the hot rocks. We sat on benches with steam rising from the rocks and the smell of dry, hot cedar stinging our noses. After we sat and sweated long enough, we slapped ourselves, and each other, with the cedar boughs Grandpa had cut, then soaped, rinsed, and dried ourselves. We had no trouble sleeping after that wonderful sauna!

Whenever Grandma or Grandpa pulled back the heavy curtain that served as their bedroom door, all I could see inside was darkness. To add to Grandma's quiet mystique, my mother warned us children to never, ever, go into Grandma's bedroom. "Don't even peek through the curtain," she told us. "That's a private room."

Every day about mid-afternoon, Grandma pulled loaves of fresh, fragrant flatbread from the oven of her big wood stove, and the bountiful smell wafted out the windows and drew me into the house. She brought out a crock of home-churned butter from the cool pantry and set it on the long oak table. Then she brought out a cold pitcher of thick, fresh cream from the icebox, and a pint jar of apple butter from the cupboard, and slowly and quietly set them on the table.

As she took cups and saucers from the cupboard, the men, who had stopped their farm work, came into the house, dirty, tired, and grim from trying to eke out a living from nothing but sand and rock. They pumped cold water into the white enamel basin on the washstand, and washed their hands. Grandpa washed first, then, in turn, each of their three grown sons washed. Uncle Glen, being the last to wash, was responsible for dumping the dirty water into the pail beneath the washstand.

The men sat around the table, poured cream and dropped sugar lumps into their coffee, and selected a spoon from the spoon glass and stirred. They slathered that cold butter, beaded with sweat from the summer heat, and some sweet fragrant apple butter, onto thick slices of warm bread and ate as if it was nothing special.

Mom brought out bread with apple butter for us children. "Take care of the girls, Connie," she always said as she poured us each of glass of lemonade.

As that summer wore on, my desire for a relationship with my grandmother grew. I could understand a few words in Finnish— but couldn't speak any, except a couple of swear words Lee had taught me. One day when I brought the plates and glasses back into the house, Grandma was standing in front of the cook stove. "Thank you for the bread, Grandma. It sure was good," I told her.

She looked past me and said something to Uncle Harvey in Finnish. Harvey got up from the table and reached past me for the teakettle, took it to the pump, and began filling it with water. Grandma walked back to the cupboard, forgetting I was even there.

Incessant buzzing of a fly caught my attention, and I looked at a flypaper strip hanging from the ceiling near the window. The sticky light brown paper had already trapped hundreds of flies. The more recent victim tried desperately to release himself from the honey-colored substance, buzzing relentlessly. Grandma ignored the fly too. I went back outside.

Later that week when Grandma was kneading bread at the table I went up to her and said, "Hello, Grandma." She turned and looked at me with such a questioning look that it frightened me, and I turned and ran from the room. When Lee saw me crying I told him, "Grandma won't talk to me."

"Aw, don't let that bother you. She don't speak English good. She don't talk to me neither."

But it did bother me. So later I decided I wasn't going to give up. I was going to get Grandma's attention somehow. I would just have to watch for the right time.

One evening I watched Grandma take the bun out of her hair and decided that was the right time. I worked up enough courage to point to her hairbrush and ask, "Can I brush your hair, Grandma?"

Grandma's eyes widened in surprise when I spoke to her. She looked at me for a few moments and then smiled, gently shook her head, and began brushing her own hair.

The next day she must have felt badly about refusing my request because she beckoned me into her bedroom. I looked at Mom for permission and Mom nodded her head. I followed Grandma through the heavily curtained doorway into her mysterious room.

Grandma sat on the side of her bed and patted a spot for me to sit next to her. I was surprised that the room was so small and that the only furniture, other than the bed, was a dresser and a wooden chair. The bedspread was a handmade quilt of dark-colored woolen squares tied at intervals with woolen yarn. A dark, worn, wool braided rug beneath our feet was starting to come apart between some of the braids.

I looked at Grandma and she looked at me. Then she reached into the top dresser drawer and took out a piece of peppermint candy. She handed it to me. I said, "Thank you," and put it in my mouth. We looked at each other again. I smiled. If only Grandma could speak English, I'd ask her about my Father in Heaven. She would know all about Him. Her daddy was a preacher.

Grandma patted my leg and said, *"Sino olet hyva tytto."* I smiled again, knowing that she had just told me that I'm a good girl. She patted my leg a couple more times and got up. I followed her out through the curtain back into the kitchen.

I had been in Grandma's bedroom! She gave me candy! She told me that I'm a good girl! I hugged that knowledge close to me like a secret for many days before I bragged to Lee about it.

But an idea had come to me after that visit. If Grandma can't speak English, then I'll learn to speak Finnish. I knew that my uncle Richard was the only one who might possibly teach me Finnish. He did most of the farming, and he was the only one who paid any attention to us children. I waited for an opportune time and said, "Uncle Richard, will you teach me to speak Finnish?"

He looked at me with astonishment in his eyes. "You don't want to talk Finn," he said. "That's for old people."

"Yes, I do," I insisted.

"Nooo," he said, stretching out the word as his eyes evaluated me. "It would take too long. You're moving to town pretty soon, anyway." With that, he got up and walked away, my hopes dragging behind him. I knew no one else would teach me.

After my visit with Grandma, our relationship went back to being almost the same as it had been—I was there, but except for an occasional smile, I wasn't acknowledged. I didn't have the close connection to my grandmother for which I longed.

Almost fifty years later, I came home one day with yet another armload of old woolen coats to tear apart, wash, sort by color, and store away in boxes until I use them to make rugs or quilts. My mother, who lived with us, said to me, "You and your grandmother! Both crazy about wool!"

"I didn't know Grandma liked wool," I said. Grandma had died shortly after I was married.

"*Like* wool?" Mom replied. "My mother was never happy unless she was spinning her wool, or carding that dirty wool they sheared off the sheep she raised. She was *crazy* about wool."

I was astounded. "I never knew Grandma spun her own wool."

"Of course you did," Mom insisted. "She knitted practically all our clothes while we were growing up."

I knew Grandma knitted, but I had only seen her knitting skeins of purchased wool. Mom then realized that by the time I knew my Grandmother, she no longer raised sheep or spun her own wool. But she had continued to knit as long as she lived. "She *had* to have her wool," Mom concluded. "That must be where you get that from."

I cannot begin to explain the feeling that went through me! A possible explanation, finally, for why I haunt secondhand stores and buy all the wool I can find, how excited I feel when I can use even a little wool in a quilt, and how much I love the feel of wool in my hands as I braid a woolen rug. I'm like my grandmother.

About a week later, while I worked at sewing a woolen quilt, I suddenly remembered that woolen quilt on my grandmother's bed—the quilt I sat on that day Grandma singled me out and made me feel special. I had completely forgotten about it.

At least, I thought I had.

CHAPTER SIXTEEN

A DAY IN TOWN

After working a seasonal job on the highway, Dad got a year-round job at Haber's Garage in Park Rapids. "Can I please go into town with Dad and spend the day?" I implored my mother over and over that long, lonely summer. I had nothing to do but watch my little sisters. The closest neighbors were miles away, and I didn't know them anyway. The only reading materials in Grandpa's house were newspapers written in Finnish, a language I couldn't read. Listening to the radio was strictly limited. Lee was always off somewhere with Glen doing *boy* things. I was lonely and bored.

Some days we visited with my Uncle Arlie's widow, Aunt Fran, and her three little girls who lived in a small house a few miles from my grandparents' home. That still left me out because Fran's daughters were the same ages as my three sisters. Donna played with Shirley, Judie played with Penny, and Irene played with Terry. The only difference was that now I was responsible for watching all six of them.

Sometimes I organized plays or performances or games that included all of them. We spent lots of time singing country western songs that we heard on Grandpa's radio. I actually thought we were pretty good when we sang the Hank Williams songs, "Kaw-Liga," "Your Cheatin' Heart," and "Hey, Good Lookin.'" Sometimes I sneaked around and listened to my Aunt Fran and Mom talking as they smoked cigarettes and drank coffee at the kitchen table. But most of the time I was just left to myself.

A few times Lee and Uncle Glen allowed me to come to the river with them to swim. The river bridge was about a mile away and a wonderful place to jump into the water. I couldn't swim, but it was fun to play in the water, except for the leeches that stuck to my legs. Lee called me a baby, but he always picked them off of me, for which I was extremely grateful. But most of the time they wouldn't let me go with them, so I was trying to convince Mom to let me go into town. "It isn't safe for a young girl to be alone all day," Mom said. I persisted. Finally she agreed to let me go.

Even as I write this I am amazed at what a small part Dad played in our lives. It would never occur to me to ask Dad if I could go with him. Mom made all the decisions. I imagine that she discussed it with Dad before she said I could go, but why wouldn't I have asked Dad directly if I could go with him?

My appointed big day in town arrived. I wore my only dress, a light blue short-sleeved cotton dress with a white shawl collar and buttons to the waist. I curled my hair, polished my saddle shoes, and left that morning feeling as if I looked almost pretty.

It felt deliciously special to be the only one going into town with Dad. I had a little money and a sack lunch, and I sat in the front seat with Dad—I had never sat in the front seat before. "What are you going to do all day?" Dad asked me.

"I don't know," I said. "I'll probably get an ice cream cone at Driscoll's, and go to the park and the beach. Should I come back at noon and eat lunch with you?"

"No, I don't know when I'll get back to the shop when I'm delivering. I don't want you waiting around for me."

"Okay," I said as my daydream about having a *lunch date with Dad* collapsed.

"Just be careful, and don't get into any trouble," Dad admonished me. He drove to Haber's Garage where he did minor mechanical jobs and delivered fuel oil to customers. "Be back here before six o'clock when I'm done for the day," Dad said as we both got out of the car, lunches in hand.

"I will," I called back to him as I quickly made my way toward Main Street.

I spent the whole day wandering around town, window-shopping at various stores, reading romance magazines at the library, and sitting at the beach. I sipped a leisurely cherry Coke while sitting on a round silver and green stool at the counter of Schneider's soda fountain and was lucky enough to get a "free" slip in my five-cent ice cream cone at Driscoll's Café and Bus Stop.

I went back to Driscoll's again in the afternoon for my free ice cream cone. While the cones were sort of papery, they were unique and almost addicting. The ice cream also tasted different, but they were the best ice cream cones, ever.

It was a hot, sunny day, and I sat alone in the shade at the edge of the beach in dress and shoes, wishing I had a swimsuit so I could cool off in the water. I took off my shoes and stockings and wiggled my feet in the cool sand. I watched young boys showing off for girls whom they thought might be watching them. Warm bodies lying all around me exuded a wonderful smell of suntan lotion that I had never smelled before. I loved it.

Later I sat swinging at the school playground and just enjoying being alone and free of responsibility. After a while, I walked toward the fisheries dam. Three boys, who were a few years older than my twelve years, started talking to me, asking me questions, and walking with me. I was pleased to have someone to talk with, and spend time with, as the day was beginning to get a little long. When we got to an area that was sort of secluded they began to make suggestive remarks. I turned and started to walk away from them, but one of them pushed me down into a ditch and jumped on me. He started to kiss and fondle me, egged on by his friends.

As he began to unbutton my dress I hit him and told him repeatedly to stop. He was big and strong, and I was no match for him. The others began saying they wanted a turn. I screamed, but no one was near enough to hear me.

The boy on top of me put one hand over my mouth and pushed my dress up to my waist with the other hand. One of the other boys grabbed my hands and held them over my head. *Father in Heaven, help me,* I silently implored as I desperately tried to think of a way out of my predicament. When the boy on top of me took his hand from my mouth in order to further undress me with both hands, I quickly said, "I have my period, and if you get that blood on you, you'll get an infection."

He let go of me. "Let's get out of here," one of the other guys said, and they all ran from me as if I had become toxic.

I sat up and rearranged my clothing with shaky hands. *Where had those words come from? Infection?* I realized that only my Father in Heaven knew the words that would turn the tide on the tragedy that was about to befall me. I still didn't know much about sex, but I knew that whatever I had been saved from would have been very bad. The boys had become a pack of hungry wolves, and I was their prey.

As I stood up out of the ditch and smoothed my hair, I kept thinking about the words that had saved me, and guilt enveloped me. I hadn't talked to my Father in Heaven for most of the summer. "Thank you, dear Heavenly Father, for saving me today," I prayed. "I'm so sorry that I haven't talked to you for so long. I do love you. Thank you. Thank you."

Of course I didn't tell my parents, or anyone, what almost happened to me that day. After we moved into town and I attended school there, I often saw those three boys. They were not bad boys, and I hope they realized later what terrible trouble they could have caused for themselves if they had not believed me.

And I think of the terrible trouble I could have been in without the words my Father in Heaven put into my mouth that day.

CHAPTER SEVENTEEN

LIFE IN A SMALL TOWN

After living with my grandparents all summer, we moved into the town of Park Rapids. We first rented a house on Riverside Avenue, and then moved to first a small, and then a larger, house owned by Ada McMahon. Mom always made it a point to leave a house cleaner and in better condition than it was when we moved in, so Ada was pleased with us as renters.

Nothing much had changed. Each rented house had wallpaper that clashed with the linoleum floor color. If we were lucky, the linoleum wasn't worn down to the black backing in the heavy traffic areas. The cloth Mom put over the sofa to cover worn spots was always a print that didn't match whatever curtains she was able to find to fit the windows.

If Mom had ever cared for aesthetics, it must have made her indescribably unhappy to keep moving to one rented house after another without money to buy what looked good in the new space. Maybe she cared a lot—and maybe that's why she apparently gave up caring altogether.

With each move to a new location, I was the one who called the electric and gas companies. I was the one who went to the grocery store for our hamburger and to the bakery for day-old bread. I was the one who bathed younger sisters in the big washtub in the middle of the kitchen and made them corn husk dolls to play with. I was the one who ironed clothes, mended clothes, took the little girls to wherever they needed to go, and helped make meals and clean up afterward. In short, I didn't have a childhood. I was always a mother.

I came home right after school and helped Mom. Frugality was the watchword. We washed plastic bags and dried them on wooden spoons standing in a glass and smoothed out used aluminum foil for reuse. We put every little piece of string on a ball so we always had string when we needed it. We used oleomargarine instead of butter.

That doesn't mean that I didn't do my share of arguing with my siblings for the honor of squeezing the color bubble in the oleomargarine bag and working it with my hands until the entire plastic bag of margarine was one smooth yellow color. We children all loved doing that. It was amazing to watch the thick orange paste from the bubble in the center slowly change the white oleo margarine into that appetizing light yellow, as we massaged the bag over and over.

⁓

I loved my sixth grade teacher that year at Park Rapids. Her name was Mrs. Jane Taig. She was gentle and patient and complimentary when I did good work. My Aunt Fran told me that when I was only three years old, she and I had sat on the front steps of Grandpa's house together and conversed like two adults. "I want to learn everything about everything," I had told her. That year in Mrs. Taig's class I felt that urge again.

I excelled at reading and writing and spelling. Mrs. Taig told me about the spelling bee and said that since I was such a good speller I should enter the competition. So I did, and I won. Then

I competed in the District Spelling Bee, but lost. It was exciting to compete, though.

My best friends that year were Patty Crowell and Avis Eno. I always felt a little envious of Avis because she was tiny and cute. Patty was more my size and I felt more comfortable with her. I did less comparing myself to her, I guess.

My first job was babysitting for the children of Mr. Murray, one of my teachers. I earned twenty-five cents an hour. I awakened from the couch when the parents came home, put on my coat, and shivered in the cold car all the while Mr. Murray drove me home. I especially remember how good that money felt in my hand—a crisp dollar bill and quarters so shiny and heavy. I never had an allowance, or money of my own, until I began earning it myself. Earning money made me feel powerful.

I saved that money and went to movies on Saturday afternoons with my brother. I looked older than twelve and was often questioned when I asked for the fifteen-cent children's fare. That made me angry, but I always refused to pay more than the rate to which I was entitled.

Judie didn't have a doll that fall and she wanted one. I made a cloth head and arms and asked Lee to cut armholes into the sides of an empty cone-shaped milk carton. I stuffed the carton with rags so it would keep its shape. Then I stuffed the head into the top of the cone, leaving a tail in the cone. I pulled the tail out of one armhole and tied it to the middle of the arm section before I ran the fabric arms through the holes. Then I cut strips of fabric for hair and drew on a face and fingernails. Judie loved her doll.

Unlike many children today, I had the security of a mother who was always home, a father who brought home a paycheck most weeks, and a home in a small town where no one ever locked their doors. I had felt the drumbeat of the high school band on parade throbbing through my veins, the exhilaration of a Tilt-A-

Whirl ride at the county fair, and the freedom to go wherever I wanted to wander. And, I was in love with the magical world of movies.

Yet responsibilities grew as I got older, and I was always Mother's Helper.

CHAPTER EIGHTEEN

STANDING ON THE THRESHOLD

"**H**urry to the bakery now, before all the day-old bread is gone," Mom said one Saturday morning as I pulled on my winter boots. Outside, in the first light of morning, I ran past Old Jake's little trailer house, my boots crunching on the snow. I cut through the alley of the big brick creamery, slowing down only a little to admire the white steam escaping from the huge soot-covered stacks. It made my breath vapor look insignificant. When I ran around the corner of the old gray hotel and came onto Main Street I gasped in awe. The Christmas lights were up! Green garlands, red bows, and colored lights canopied the center of town and decorated the light posts as far as I could see. A light frost softened the ethereal scene.

Our sixth grade class had been studying countries that don't have snow in winter. My imaginative mind envisioned the scene before me as a Christmas card, the edges covered with glittering snow and me in the middle of the card, standing on Main Street wishing everyone a Merry Christmas. I would send the card to all the kids in those other countries so they could enjoy the wintry beauty of Christmas, 1953, at Park Rapids, Minnesota.

My weekly errand to the bakery took me past the stale cigarette smell of the pool hall (which I was never, ever, to go into), Wimpy's Café (that always smelled of fried onions and hamburgers), National Tea Grocery, Severson's Appliance, and Walsh's Coast-to-Coast. When I reached the new window display of shiny toys and gifts at Walsh's Hardware, I forgot I was in a hurry. Right in the middle front of the window sat the most beautiful bride doll I had ever seen. She had real eyelashes, and eyes that opened and closed, and a little red smiling mouth that showed real teeth. Her dress was white satin with tiny pearl buttons, and the headdress on her white veil was decorated with lilies of the valley. The veil hung down over her blonde hair like a real bride. She even had little white shoes and stockings. I stood there quite a long time before I remembered my errand. *The bakery!*

With two bags of day-old bread in my arms I stopped once again in front of the bride doll. I knew my mother and father could never afford to buy me such an expensive Christmas gift, and my older brother Lee had given me the bad news about Santa Claus a couple years ago, so what could I hope for? Nothing! I knew I could never have this beautiful doll.

But I wanted her more than anything I had ever wanted—even more than the fingernail polish I had been trying to convince Mom and Dad that I was old enough to wear. Maybe if I told Mom how much I really wanted this doll, maybe she could get her for me for Christmas. But I knew they couldn't afford it. But maybe I should tell her about the doll anyway, just in case. Maybe, just maybe …

Mom took the bag of bread from me when I got home. She seemed upset about something. "You girls stop running in the house," she yelled at my three little sisters. She reached out her long arms and quickly wiped Irene's nose with a hanky produced from her apron pocket. With a quick kiss on Irene's cheek she turned and said in a tired voice, "Lee, stop picking at the oilcloth.

You'll wear a hole in it. I can't afford to buy a new one this week."

If Mom couldn't even afford to buy a new oilcloth for the table, she sure couldn't afford to buy that doll for me. Tears threatened to fall as quickly as my hopes had just fallen, and I rushed to the bedroom I shared with my three sisters.

Every day after that, I met my two little sisters after school and we walked the long way home so I could look at the bride doll. One night I had an idea. Maybe I could save enough babysitting money to buy the doll. I usually spent that money on afternoon movies. I loved the movies, but I loved that bride doll even more. I decided to start saving my money.

A few weeks later, my sisters were looking at the Sears and Roebuck catalog, showing Mom what they wanted Santa to bring them. "What would you like for Christmas, Connie?" Mom asked me.

"Connie wants the bride doll in the hardware store," Donna said.

"Is that true? You want a bride doll?" Mom asked with a surprised look.

"She makes us go there every day so she can look at her," Judie added.

I didn't want Mom to feel badly because she couldn't afford to buy me the doll, and I didn't know what to say to her. "Aren't you a little too old to play with dolls?" Mom asked.

"She isn't for playing with," I said. "She's just for looking at." I didn't expect her to understand how important she was to me. I didn't know, myself, why I had such a burning desire to have that doll at the very time I was trying to convince Mom and Dad that I was grown up enough to wear fingernail polish. My head and my heart were clearly at odds with each other. "I know she's too expensive. I'm going to save my babysitting money and I'll buy her myself," I said. "I already have a dollar seventy-five cents saved."

The next Monday when we went to see my bride doll after school, she wasn't in the window. I panicked. *Maybe they brought her inside.* I went into the store holding tightly to both my sisters' hands. "Where is the bride doll from the window?" I asked with a trembling voice.

"We sold her this morning," the clerk said. "Do you want to see something else?"

I could barely get out the door before I began crying. My sisters looked at me in silence and tried hard to keep up as I almost ran from the store. I couldn't stop crying until we were almost home. "Maybe Santa Claus will bring you a bride doll," Donna said.

"Maybe," I said, knowing better, as I wiped away my tears. "Don't tell Mom I was crying because the doll is gone. I'm going to say I fell and hurt my knee. I know I'm not supposed to lie, but I don't want Mom to feel bad, so I have to tell her something so she won't feel bad, okay?" My sisters looked at me with large eyes and nodded. I knew they'd keep my secret.

The Friday afternoon before Christmas our school had a Christmas program. I was both excited and nervous as I dressed in costume for the Christmas play. I knew Dad would be delivering fuel oil, earning his fifty dollars a week that I heard Mom say was not enough to raise five children on, but at least Mom could come see me playing the Christmas angel. I had overheard Mrs. McMahon telling Mom she could ride to school with her. When I peeked out from behind the curtain I couldn't find Mom in the audience. After Mrs. McMahon drove us home I said, "Mom, why didn't you come see our play?"

"I didn't have any way to get there," she said, looking down as her long, thin fingers worked her needle in and out of the patch she was sewing on Dad's overalls.

"Mrs. McMahon was there. She said you could ride with her," I said, not understanding.

"I just couldn't make it, honey. I'm sorry."

"I had the lead part. I wanted you to see me."

"I know. I'm sorry."

"Well, why didn't you come?" I continued, hurt that she hadn't seen me play such an important part.

"I didn't have anything to wear. Okay? I just didn't have anything to wear," Mom whispered. She dropped the overalls on the chair and walked away in tears.

I felt terrible. "Heavenly Father," I prayed, "please make Mom happy at Christmas." I spent my babysitting money and bought Mom a small blue bottle of Evening in Paris perfume and wrapped it in blue tissue paper to match the bottle. I wanted her to have something special on Christmas Eve.

After supper we began to open our gifts from under the tree. First Irene pulled the paper from a colorful top that made her shriek with delight when it spun around. Next Judie opened her present and found a big, fat coloring book and a new box of Crayola crayons. Donna was delighted with her hand puppet. Then it was my turn.

I carefully undid the tape and opened the wrapping paper to find a small cedar box with a little brass latch. Inside the box were a bottle of pink nail polish and a bottle of nail polish remover. "Oh, Mom!" I said, looking at her with gratitude. I knew she had convinced Dad to let me wear nail polish. "Thanks, Dad," I said, giving him a hug before I went to hug Mom. *She does know I'm not a child anymore.* That meant as much to me as the nail polish itself.

Mom didn't look pleased when she opened my gift to her. She said, "Thank you," but I could tell she didn't like it. Later I said, "Mom, don't you like your present?"

She looked at me and said, "You spent a lot of money on that perfume. Why didn't you spend that money for something I needed?"

"I wanted you to feel pretty," I told her.

She snorted in disgust and said, "Who has time to feel pretty around here? That takes time and money, and I don't have either. Next time, buy me something practical."

I always did well at home and at school and always got As on my report cards. Now, I felt as if Mom had just handed me a big, fat, red F. Fs don't feel good.

After the gifts were opened we played card games while we listened to Christmas music on the radio and ate salted-in-the-shell peanuts that Dad had brought home as a special Christmas treat. Mom didn't put on any of the perfume.

Mom has been gone for many years now and I am a great-grandmother myself, but when I see a cobalt blue Evening in Paris perfume bottle in an antique store I still feel the sting of that rejected gift so very long ago.

That Christmas Eve, we hung up our stockings and went to bed early, eager for Christmas morning. Donna, Judie, and Irene prayed for what they hoped Santa would put under the tree for them. I felt so bad about making Mom cry, and now I felt even worse because she didn't like my Christmas gift. My prayer was only that my Heavenly Father would make Mom happy on Christmas Day.

Early the next morning my sisters tugged at me. "Wake up, Connie. Let's go downstairs and see what Santa brought." I followed them down the narrow, wooden stairs and across the cold linoleum kitchen floor, my bare feet tingling. Ahead I heard the squeals of excitement from the living room. "Look what I got! Look what I got!" they all said as they jumped up and down with the joy and magic of a mystical Santa and their new toys. I glanced at their toys and then my still-sleepy eyes sought my own designated spot under the tree.

I couldn't believe what I saw! There, in all her gorgeous white finery, sat my bride doll. Mom had bought her for me even though …? I reached down and carefully picked her up. When I turned around Mom was standing in the doorway, tying her old pink chenille robe around her thin waist, smiling at me. The look of pure pleasure on her face when she saw my surprise and happiness made her sacrifice acceptable to me. And she was happy! My love for her at that moment was inexpressible, and my love for my Heavenly Father overflowed!

These many years later, my bride doll's gown and veil have yellowed, but she's still beautiful. When I look at her, she reminds me of yet one more time when my Heavenly Father heard my prayers and gave me what I needed. And I can once again see the joy on my mother's face as she sacrificed her own needs for me that Christmas of 1953 when I stood with one foot over the threshold of becoming a young woman while the other foot lingered in my childhood.

CHAPTER NINETEEN

ADVICE

Things My Mother Told Me

- Stick to yourself.
- Don't have anything to do with the neighbors.
- We're poor, so we're not as good as other people. They don't want to have anything to do with us.
- Just because we're poor doesn't mean we have to be dirty or ragged.
- Don't ask for anything. We can't afford it.
- Don't waste anything.
- Whenever we get clothes from someone else, ask:
1. Will it fit one of us?
2. Can we alter it to fit one of us?
3. Can we make something else to wear from it?
4. Can we use it to patch other clothing?
5. If not, can we cut it up for quilts or rugs?
6. If not, can we use it for cleaning rags?
- Always cut off the buttons and zippers so we can use them again.

- Write grocery lists on the back of old envelopes to save paper.
- Take the worn collar off a shirt, turn it over, sew it back on, the shirt will look new again.
- Clean your plate; it's a sin to waste food.
- Don't take more than you can eat.
- Work first, then play.
- Always get into the corners when you clean.
- It doesn't pay to sweep the kitchen floor if you don't also sweep the sand from the front steps.
- Many hands make light work.
- Always carry a dime for a phone call.
- Keep yourself neat and clean.
- Always sit with your knees together.
- Always carry a hanky.
- Always wear clean underwear.
- Stand up straight.
- Sit up straight.
- Work at having good penmanship.
- Be polite to others.
- Respect other people's property.
- Always wait to be asked.
- Never steal.
- Always be honest.
- Never cheat.
- If you can't say anything good about someone, don't say anything at all.
- Don't talk back to adults.
- Respect your elders.
- Don't ever let boys touch your breasts. It causes cancer.
- Never go all the way with a boy, or a decent man will never marry you.
- Take care of your sisters.

I know that Mom was imparting knowledge she believed I would need to survive in the world as she understood it. She did the best she could with what she knew. And I have passed on many of these same adages to my own children, knowing them to be important in the formation of honest, productive people. Yet I often have longed for other advice that would have helped to shape me into a more self-confident, more caring, and considerate person.

It makes me wonder what things I don't know, that I should be telling my children.

Things I Wish My Mother Had Told Me

- To develop a sense of humor.
- To have consideration for others.
- That there are others less fortunate than us.
- That I can accomplish anything I want to do.
- To think positively.
- To be generous to others with both time and money.
- To not be afraid to fail.
- To seek adventure without fear.
- To handle money wisely.
- To set goals and believe I can reach them.
- That I am just as good as everyone else.
- That God loves me, and so does she.

CHAPTER TWENTY

MOVIES, KISSING, AND WINNING CONTESTS

I loved going to the movies when I was young, and still do. It is an opportunity to immerse oneself in another world—into the minds and hearts of other people. When I was twelve, the Orpheum Theatre at Park Rapids sold the dregs of the popcorn called *old maids* for a penny a box. Lee and I always bought the old maids because that's what we could afford. They tasted wonderful to us.

Some of the movie stars I adored were Grace Kelly, Audrey Hepburn, Ingrid Bergman, Deborah Kerr, Gloria Grahame, Joan Crawford, Anne Baxter, Jane Wyman, Loretta Young, Gary Cooper, Yul Brynner, Clark Gable, Humphrey Bogart, Frank Sinatra, Marlon Brando, and William Holden.

Some of the movies I especially enjoyed that year were *The King and I*, starring Yul Brynner; *The Ten Commandments,* starring Charlton Heston; and *From Here to Eternity,* starring Deborah Kerr.

Looking older than my age sometimes came in handy. The following year during the summer celebration at Park Rapids, I lied about my age and got a job selling tickets to the merry-go-round. I sat in a little booth all day listening to the merry-go-round music. I loved feeling so grown up, taking people's money, making change, and giving out tickets. It was a good two days.

When I was in seventh grade, some little kids were playing on the merry-go-round at the school playground and an older boy was harassing them. After watching for a while, I got angry and told the boy to quit picking on the little kids. Then he started in on me.

His name was Alfred Anderson and it turned out he wasn't really a bad kid. He became my boyfriend. We sat at basketball games together and then he walked me home. We held hands and stopped to kiss each other frequently. For Christmas, Alfred gave me a gold heart necklace with my name on the front and his name on the back. I still have it.

We met often at the dam bridge and kissed. When I went home I always wondered whether anyone could tell by looking at me that I had been kissing a boy. I remember one day in particular when I sat with my sisters on the bench outside of Old Jake's trailer house, thinking that I must be wearing my feelings on my face for the whole world to see. Did my Heavenly Father know how I felt about kissing? Was it okay to like kissing boys? I didn't know.

I believed then, and still do, as does Julia Roberts, that kissing is highly under-rated. In fact, I've been intrigued by kissing ever since I saw older boys kissing girls in the cloakroom at the Orrock schoolhouse, and ever since my distant relative kissed me in the back of the pickup truck.

Earlier that spring, the Chamber of Commerce held a contest at school for children to sell buttons, with the proceeds going to buy trees to be planted at the airport. I sold the most buttons and won the contest. The prize was a free weekend at a cabin in Canada with the president of the Chamber of Commerce and his family. This was huge for someone like me who never got the opportunity to go to a lake cabin or travel to fun places. On the appointed weekend I rode to St. Francis, Ontario, with the president and his family. From there we took a boat across the water to their cabin on an island. Such fun! We fished and ate and sat around a bonfire at night and told stories and laughed. It was all new and wonderful to me.

The cabin was rustic. An outhouse sat upon a hill not far from the cabin. They had other guests there that weekend, as well. My host had installed an intercom directly behind the back wall of the outhouse. When a couple of the women went up the hill to the outhouse, our host growled into the intercom like a mean, angry bear. Of course it sounded to the women as if the bear was behind them. The women ran down the hill screaming—one of them forgetting to pull up her pants. The men thought it was hilarious. I didn't.

Today when I drive to Park Rapids, I can't see any trees that may have been planted at the airport in 1954. Did the airport move? Did the trees die over the past fifty years? Have I outlived them? Where is the result of those many hours I walked the streets of Park Rapids saying, "Will you please buy a button and help plant a tree, mister? Only fifty cents."

I became ill with pneumonia the year that I was thirteen. I was hospitalized for over a week. Lee came to see me one day and brought me a music magazine. Back then, music magazines were popular—sort of a cross between a comic book and a movie magazine. One of the articles was about Patti Page, a popular singer. It included a contest. In twenty-five words or less, we were to write why we like the Patti Page Mama Doll song. The prize was a Patti Page Mama Doll. I entered the contest from the hospital—I had nothing else to do—and won the contest. I received a beautiful doll with blonde Saran hair, blue eyes, and a banner that read, "Patti Page Mama Doll." The maker was the Roberta Doll Company.

Many years later, I took the doll to a Patti Page concert at Orchestra Hall in Minneapolis. When Patti came into the audience singing a medley and shaking hands with people, from my aisle seat, I lifted the doll to show her. She stopped singing and asked, "Where did you get that? I don't have a doll like that." Then she realized that she had stopped singing. She looked to the music director, who began again and she whispered, "See me after the show." I did and got wonderful pictures of us together with the doll. I had a permanent ink pen with me and she wrote on the cloth body of the doll, "Connie, thank you for remembering, Patti Page 1987."

That is the doll I treasure second most in my doll collection. My bride doll is still my favorite.

Of course, it was not long before my father decided to move again. We moved to Aldrich Avenue in North Minneapolis, and Dad started working at Fry Roofing Company earning ninety-nine cents an hour.

It was summer, and Lee quickly made a few friends. Lee Anderson and Owen Fagerman were two of the first friends he made. I was trying to get used to living in a large city. It was noisy and crowded, and most of the time I just wanted to be someplace by myself. But some of us kids in the neighborhood got together in the evenings and played Spin the Bottle. Of course, that meant kissing boys. I loved that game. Kissing really was my thing.

CHAPTER TWENTY-ONE

WHITE GIRL LEARNS A LESSON

One day a visiting pastor of a nearby church convinced my mother that Lee and I should attend confirmation classes. So Lee and I went to the next class and got our books. We were in seventh and eighth grades, and the other students were much younger. Yet everyone else knew things about the Bible that we didn't know. They laughed when we hadn't heard about the Ten Commandments. They howled when we didn't know the Lord's Prayer. We felt dumb and completely out of place. That was a new feeling for me—the smart one—and I didn't like it one bit.

The pastor heaped past lessons upon current lessons for us so we could catch up. None of what we were studying seemed to relate to my Heavenly Father except the Lord's Prayer. And Lee didn't even have that much to go on. I started to tell him about my Heavenly Father when we were coming home after a class one day, but he was so frustrated he couldn't even listen to any more "religion." So I dropped the subject.

I wondered whether I could ask the pastor some of my burning questions, but he was always so eager to have us leave when class was over that I felt it to be an imposition if I asked to talk to him.

Besides, Lee wouldn't want to wait while I talked to the pastor. *I'll wait until I get to know him better, then I'll ask if there is only one Father in Heaven or if everyone has their own Father. I'll ask him how my Heavenly Father can see me all the time. Does He know what I'm thinking all the time? How can I hear His answer if I ask Him a question?* I wanted to discuss so many things with someone who had the answers, but it would have to wait.

Lee and I became more frustrated with the classes. I wasn't usually a party to the unconventional things Lee was prone to do on a sort of regular basis, but this time I conspired along with him. After a few weeks of attending confirmation classes, we went to church early on class day, dropped off our books, and never returned. "Dear Father in Heaven," I said that night in bed, "I'm sorry, but I just couldn't do it. I'm sorry. I still love you. I hope you still love me." Mom never said anything to us about not going.

⟨⟩

During those early years in the city, Mom took us girls to her sister Alice's house a couple times a year, and Alice gave our hair a permanent wave. Alice was my mother's youngest sister. When I was a baby, Alice fed me sweetened whipped cream because I liked it so much. No wonder I was a chubby little baby. As I got a little older, she always told me that I looked just like the child movie star Shirley Temple. She curled my hair in long ringlets like Shirley wore.

Alice was a hairdresser, and she always had her hair styled nicely, and she wore pretty clothes. She wore White Shoulders perfume, so she smelled nice too. It was with both joy and trepidation that I went to Aunt Alice's on those occasions.

Alice had a cheerful house with yellow curtains at her kitchen windows. She always had bakery donuts and sweet rolls on the table when we got there on Saturday morning. Such a rare treat. And she had a television set, so we watched *Hopalong Cassidy* and *Ramah of the Jungle*. Another rare treat.

But when it was my turn for a haircut and a perm, I cringed because Alice was so rough. She was busy talking to Mom and when she wanted me to turn my head, she just grabbed my hair and pulled it to turn me the way she wanted me to turn. I have a sensitive scalp. After my sessions with Aunt Alice, my head was sore for a week.

That fall, Lee and I started seventh grade together at Franklin Junior High. Somewhere along the way, Lee was held back a year and we were in the same grade. It must have been because of his lack of interest in school, because it certainly was not his lack of intelligence. At Franklin, the student body was about one-third black, one-third Hispanic, and one-third white. What a culture shock for a small-town girl who had never even seen a black person before.

I was, once again, the new girl and the focus of attention. Only this time the guys were black and Hispanic as well as white, and I didn't know how to interact with them. They looked different. They walked different. They talked different. They even smelled different. I didn't dislike the difference; I just didn't know how to treat them the same when they were so different. They sensed that and reacted to me with profanity in language and actions.

The girls even acted differently. Girls weren't supposed to use profanity. Girls weren't supposed to fight with each other. I was clearly out of my element, and they knew it and used it against me.

Furthermore, the girls were jealous of the attention the boys were giving me. When I look back at photographs of myself as a child and a young girl, I realize that I was sort of pretty. I never knew it then. I always thought I got so much attention from boys just because I was the new girl. I realize now it was partly because of how I looked. I wonder why I didn't know I was attractive. Was it because of Dad?

My earliest memory of my father is my birthday when I was very young—four or five. I was sitting in the highchair because I needed to sit up high enough so my mother didn't have to bend down to curl my hair. She was going to have a baby soon. "You're going to be so pretty," Mom told me as she took the hot curling iron off the wood cook stove behind her and caught a wet towel between its jaws briefly, letting the worst of the heat sizzle off before she caught a strand of my long, blonde hair with it. After a steady turning of the handle until the iron reached close to my scalp, she held it for a few moments. I could feel the heat on my scalp. Just as I began to cringe, afraid my head would burn, she unrolled the long curl.

"Hold still," Mom told me every time she brought the hot iron close to me. "You're going to put on that pretty blue dress that I made for you, and I'll put a ribbon in your hair, and Daddy is going to see how pretty you are. We'll go out and take him some lunch."

In my new dress, Mom and I walked out to the field with Dad's lunch. However, when we got to the field, Dad was so angry about something that wasn't going right that he hardly looked at me, even when Mom told him to look at how pretty I was.

I still remember feeling so sad that day when Daddy didn't tell me I was pretty. He never did tell me, ever, that he thought I was pretty. If your daddy doesn't think you're pretty, you must not be pretty. In my mind, that became a fact.

But, at Franklin Junior High School, I was also having a bad time because I didn't have nice clothes like most of the girls. And then we had to buy gym clothes.

I was thirteen, that age when everything your parents do in public embarrasses you. It was bad enough that I had to go to a new school again, but Mom took me to the Goodwill secondhand thrift store to buy the required tennis shoes and white-blouse-and-navy-shorts gym uniform. "We don't have money for new," Mom said repeatedly as I followed her down Broadway Avenue in North Minneapolis, protesting her choice of store.

We found what my mother decided would "make do," and my shame turned to pure mortification when the clerk pulled out a piece of newspaper to wrap our purchase. I practically ran home carrying the string-tied parcel that loudly announced our poverty to passersby.

Later, tears blurred my vision as I pulled out the navy blue hand-stitched name of the girl who wore the uniform before me.

The blouse and shorts passed muster in gym class, but the tennis shoes were not the popular flat bottom kind worn those days. Mine had a heel. Immediately the other girls started laughing at my "high-heeled tennis shoes." I wanted to cry and go home. Instead I tried to tune out their taunts. "When I grow up I will never buy anything at the Goodwill store," I said.

Paula—a tall, strong-looking, black girl—decided to beat me up because another girl, Wendy, told her I had said, "I could beat up Paula." I later learned that Wendy was jealous because her boyfriend was interested in me.

No matter how I tried to tell Paula I never said that, she was determined we were going to fight after school. Somehow I managed to avoid that altercation.

However, many of the black and Hispanic guys had started to taunt me in the hallways. One day I was walking to lunch and one of the worst offenders, a black boy named Jerome, grabbed my breast and said something nasty. I couldn't take it anymore. I hit him with my books. He hit me back. I hit him with my fists and he knocked my glasses off. I came after him and kept hitting him as hard as I could, yelling at him until a teacher pulled me away from him.

I had refused to fight with a girl, but here I was, fighting with a boy—a big black boy!

I ran, crying, to my locker to get my things. "I'm going home and never coming back," I told the teacher who finally convinced me to go into the office. The principal made Jerome apologize to me and promise to never swear around me or touch me again.

The amazing thing is after that fight I had the respect of all the other kids. If anyone said a swear word around me they would immediately say, "Oh, I'm sorry, Connie." I made many black and Hispanic friends. In fact, one of my best friends, Nancy Clark, was my biggest competitor in school. She was a beautiful, bright, black girl. One day we were walking home together when my dad came along in the car. He pulled over and sternly ordered me to get into the car. He said, "I don't ever want to see you walking on the same side of the street with a n----- again. Do you hear me?"

After that, I tried to be careful that my Dad wasn't around when I was in public with a black or Hispanic person. I wasn't going to give up my friends. Reggie and Ronnie Commodore were two black guy friends whom I remember fondly. Corrina Torres was a wonderful Hispanic friend.

Today I like to see people of other colors and cultures living into our small Minnesota town because it enriches our lives to know and understand people of other ethnic groups. While we are different, we are all so much alike.

I had thought I was the only one who, as a child, felt humiliation in our poverty. In 1995, at a weeklong writer's workshop in Duluth, I learned I was wrong. A black woman about my age wrote about that same, hollow-chested shame she felt as a teenager standing in line with her mother for a government handout.

This group of seventeen writers, meeting to write about family at Split Rock Art Center, couldn't have been more diverse in race, culture, age, and gender than if it had been orchestrated by integrationists. The more we wrote about our cultural differences, the more we discovered our inherent similarities. The seventy-year-old Hungarian Jewish woman—a Holocaust survivor—suffered because of estrangement from her daughter. A middle-aged Caucasian man, unable to bridge the silent gulf with his father, felt the same pain. The lesbian white woman wrote of the same societal victimization as did the young, black, single mother. The scarred, haunted life story written by the Greek woman raped by a teacher was the same story told by the young black woman abused by her mother.

Just as we know that no race distinction exists in a person's DNA, we found no race distinction in pain, sorrow, or joy. The Native American woman suffers the same pain of prejudice as does the black man. The young wealthy woman felt as immobilized by her family's wealth as I did by my family's poverty. Wisdom surfaced from the depths of the elderly, rural, uneducated woman the same as it did from the white, female physician and the young, black, male college professor. We all shared the same joy at capturing the essence of our own stories and creating acceptable literary work.

We were a community for a week, writing what we know and feel, gathering knowledge from each others' experiences. Our worlds expanded as we found new understanding of cultures unlike our own, yet our world became smaller in the realization that God created us all so much alike.

As I live here in Monticello, I see the same kind of effort to expand our world with global knowledge. We are fortunate to have residents of many races and cultures, so we can experience unique foods, philosophies, and traditions different from our own. Exchange students and world travel add to our comprehension. We are blessed when we come to realize the more we are different, the more we are alike. In the words of my new friend who survived the concentration camps, "If I learn to understand all people, I will never be alone."

CHAPTER TWENTY-TWO

GRADUATING

Movies were the usual date while I was in junior high. One night my date and I sat in the theatre eating popcorn, talking, and waiting for the movie to begin. When the lights dimmed and the newsreels began to roll, my date looked at me and whispered, "You're pretty in the dark."

I have laughed about that over the many years of my life. I know he meant it as a sincere compliment, but it certainly was left-handed. Whenever someone tells me I'm pretty, I want to say, "I know—in the dark."

A few weeks later, I was at the Paradise Theatre on Broadway Avenue watching *Gone With the Wind* with a date. I was enjoying it totally when the lights came on and the movie action stopped. The theatre manager announced it was almost 9:30 and anyone under the age of sixteen must leave the theatre because of the city curfew. This was a longer movie, and the first time the curfew had affected me. My date and I had to leave the theatre without seeing the end of the movie. I was crushed. I had to come back to a matinee in order to see the whole movie. I felt especially bad for my date because he was sixteen and could have stayed through the movie.

At Franklin Junior High, I went on to be elected to Student Council and class officer and was even voted "The girl with the nicest personality" in ninth grade. I sewed a pale yellow cotton dress to wear for our graduation day. Girls never wore pants of any kind to school. We always wore skirts or dresses. We wore bobby socks and saddle shoes with them. Sweater sets were popular too.

At graduation, our choir sang "I Believe." I sang alto. We had practiced for many weeks. I still smile every time I hear that song.

Although I didn't know it, at graduation I would be awarded the American Legion Award for Outstanding Student. Someone called to notify Mom of my honor and invite her to the graduation ceremony. I was more honored by Mom's attendance at the graduation ceremony that day than I was for winning the award. Mom never came to anything at school. I felt so proud of her. I introduced her to all my teachers and my friends, and I couldn't stop smiling. That night I thanked my Heavenly Father for bringing Mom to school—for giving her the courage to overcome her fears in order to please me.

That was the only school function Mom ever attended while I was in school. She wasn't comfortable with other people, feeling that she might not be dressed right or might not do or say the right thing. She always thought she was too skinny, had ugly arms, didn't have a nice hairdo, and didn't have nice enough clothes.

In actuality, Mom was a beautiful woman. Her skin was flawless. She had a natural white streak in her hair that others thought she had had done at a beauty shop because it grew right where her hair waved across the front of her face. That made her angry. "Do people think I spend money at a beauty shop when I don't even have decent clothes to wear?" she said.

By the time I was in junior high, Mom was no longer skinny, rather just nice and slim. But, like women who have eating disorders, Mom never saw herself as she was. She thought she was still skinny, refusing to wear anything sleeveless because of her "skinny arms." She had beautiful legs, but she thought they too were skinny. She was intelligent and gracious, but she didn't know that either. She was negative about everything in life, mostly herself.

Mom modeled behavior most of her life, for which I aspired to be just the opposite. Yet I look back and see how much I was like my mother when I was growing up. I didn't think I was as good as others. I didn't stand up for myself. I didn't voice my wishes. I didn't have the gumption to go after what I wanted. I didn't want to make waves. I didn't want anyone to be angry with me.

How much of that do I still carry with me? I avoid conflict; I often feel as if I am not as refined or "classy" as many of my friends; and I am not comfortable entertaining because I'm not sure I am doing everything right. A couple years ago I bought ten copies of *Etiquette for Dummies*. It was the best etiquette book I could find. I gave one to each of my four daughters, my four oldest granddaughters, and one of our "adopted" daughters. I kept one for myself. I don't want any of them to feel as unsure of what to do as I sometimes do. I know I certainly have not taught them well in that area. I hope the book makes up for it.

CHAPTER TWENTY-THREE

DAD'S FAMILY

My father was the original Archie Bunker in his actions and attitudes. Some of the things he said sounded like they came from his Kentucky hillbilly ancestors. He said "et" for "ate." He added "a" in front of words like, "It's a'raining."

Dad's father left the family when Dad was twelve, and the county took Dad and his five siblings away from his mother. Dad and his older brother, Harvey, ran from the officials before they could be taken to the orphanage. They escaped by hiding in cornfields, sleeping in culverts, and then going to Park Rapids to live with their mother's brother and his family. Later the State of Minnesota gave Dad and Harvey to their uncle, Marshall Duncan, and his wife Sarah, with an indentured servant's contract. They lived near Annandale, Minnesota.

As sad as I felt for Dad when I learned how he had been raised, I felt worse for his cousin, Harold Newman, who was taken from his home about the same time as Dad was taken from his mother. This is what Harold told me:

My teeth chattered together like it was hard winter. What if nobody is glad to see me? Nine years since they took me away from here. What if nobody remembers me? I stood at the top of Fairhaven Hill and looked at the town I was born to sixteen years ago and I thought about Ma.

Ma took sick the year I turned seven, and on her burial day I was sittin' under the back steps so everybody wouldn't keep lookin' at me all pitiful-like. I heard the church ladies say it's 1918 now and they have sanitariums in Minneapolis that could'a cured Ma. But she wouldn't leave us four boys with Pa, him being so unreliable. I didn't understand what "unreliable" meant at the time, but I figured it out when Pa drank whiskey all day and we didn't have no food to eat. My brother Walter walked on down to Uncle Roy's and said could we have some eggs. Aunt Minnie brought Walter home in the buggy with eggs and a bucket of milk too. She looked in the cupboard and then went out all mad-like to find Pa. It was after that when Pa got sobered up and went into town and come back with a big sack of flour, some salt pork, and sorghum. My brother Henry made flapjacks and fried some pork, and we ate good.

First Henry and Walter stopped going to school, and then me and Paul didn't go no more neither. The other boys helped Pa and Uncle Roy on the farm, but I was pretty little yet, so mostly I just played with my puppy Teddy. We'd go up in the hayloft so nobody'd see me cryin' and call me a baby. Teddy would lick my face and we'd lay in the hayloft and I'd try to remember some of the Bible stories Ma told me after she took to bed. "God loves you, Harold," she always said when she was done with the story. "Remember that, and be a good boy."

One day Pa said we gotta go back to school or the county would come get us, so the next day we all went back to school, but it was too late already. We was all sittin' in the schoolroom when Walter yelled somethin' at Henry and they took off like lightnin' out the back door. A big, black car was pullin' up outside, and a man got out and talked to teacher, and then grabbed me and Paul by the back of our shirts and just dragged us out and shoved us in that car. Paul was swearin and kickin at the man, but it didn't do no good.

The man took us to the sheriff's office, and sheriff said, "I'll take them home to Betsy. She'll give them a bath and a good hot meal."

We stayed at the sheriff's house for a few days, and Mrs. James washed and mended our clothes and fed us good. I didn't give them no trouble because Mrs. James made me think of Ma, but Paul weren't nice to them. He kept saying, "You can't keep us here," but he didn't try to run away or nothin'. Mostly, I just wished my dog Teddy was there too.

A few days later the sheriff took me and Paul to the courthouse and told us to just stand there. Lots of people was lookin' at us. The sheriff says, "Okay, folks, these are the boys. Both in good health. As you know, an Indentured Servant Contract means if you take one of these boys to raise, you have to see to his education through eighth grade. When he turns eighteen, you have to provide him a good suit of clothes and give him one hundred dollars, and he's free to go. Any questions?"

Then the people started lookin' us over, but nobody wanted us. The man who drove us away said it was cuz we was too little to be of use to them. He said he was takin' us to the Owatonna State School to be raised as orphans. When we got there I was glad the trip was over, but Paul wouldn't get out of the car. When the man grabbed him and pulled him out, he caught hold of the door handle and held on with both hands. Two men come out and pried at his hands while he yelled, "No, no," the whole time until they finally got him loose and into the building.

They made us take off all our clothes and they scrubbed us with something awful-smelling. Then we got cabbage soup, but Paul wouldn't eat.

We was kept in that cottage with other new kids for a few weeks to make sure we didn't have some disease, then we was each assigned to a different cottage. Brothers couldn't live together. That was their rules. We went to school, had chores to do, had playtime, and then went to bed. Every day was the same. I couldn't talk to Paul because every one of those there cottages had thirty kids and we all had to stay in our own area. I never knowed what happened to Henry and Walter.

Our matron was okay, but the two assistants was mean. Kids was always trying to escape, and when they was brought back, there was hell to pay. I jumped the train a couple times when the train loaded apples and beef from the farm. I got caught both times and the cottage assistants beat me terrible. A kid named Duane jumped train with me that last time, and they beat him so bad he couldn't never hear after that. Leastwise, as long as I was there he never could hear no more. I was scared to try again after that.

When I was twelve I was indentured out to a farmer from Morristown. I was glad to be gettin away from the orphanage. Our matron told me he was a good man and he would raise me right. I was glad to hear that cuz I heard some stories of kids who was treated real bad by those families, especially girls, who was raped and come back to the orphanage pregnant. The families always tell it like the girls went and got theirselves pregnant. But the girls say it was the fathers or the brothers that did it. Sometimes both.

I thought about Paul. Paul had been indentured about a year earlier and had smuggled a note to me before he left. I wondered now if I would be close to where he is. I never heard from Pa or my other brothers. Matron said we should forget our families, but it was hard to forget. But I'd be getting a new family now.

Mother Jensen was a kind lady, short and stout with a high-pitched voice. I was glad she didn't talk much. Father Jensen was mean and lazy. The only good thing I can say about him was that I come out big and strong because of all the hard work he forced on me.

I was up before daylight every morning to feed and milk the cows before I went to school. When I come home from school I had to clean barns and feed and milk the cows again. Father Jensen found plenty for me to do until well past bedtime every night. Sometimes I fell asleep during school and teacher had to rap me on the head with a ruler to wake me up.

During the spring and fall I had to stay home from school to do field work. Father Jensen fed the calves and the pigs and seeded the crops. I did everything else, with Father Jensen kicking and beating me much of the time. Sometimes he beat me so bad I passed out. He never give me a reason. He'd just take off his belt, real slow-like, with a grin on his face. Then he'd say, "Come here now, boy. The Good Book says 'spare the rod and spoil the child.' I got a responsibility to raise you right." Then he'd start beating me.

I ran once, but the next time he near beat me to death, so I figured I best just stand for it. Nobody ever come to check on me like I heard they was suppose to. So I never had nobody to complain to. I just had to take it.

The summer I turned sixteen I decided I weren't gonna take it no more. I started making me some plans. I had a big, old, green bicycle, and that would be my means of escape. I packed me some things in a bag and watched for the right time.

I didn't have to wait too long before Father and Mother Jensen said they was gonna visit some neighbors in the morning. Soon as they left I quick made some sandwiches, grabbed my bag, and took off in the opposite direction.

I had studied maps at school and knowed how to get to Fairhaven. It was about 120 miles away. I got myself over to Highway One and headed north, watchin' behind me all the time. When I seen a car comin' up in the distance I ducked down in the ditch till it passed. After a while I figured nobody was chasin' me so I stopped watchin'. My bicycle had big tires, and I was strong from workin' so long and hard, and I rode that bike hard and fast, not stoppin' for nothin' except to pee alongside the road once in a while and grab a sandwich from my bag.

I never knowed the countryside could be so beautiful, with so many big, fluffy, white clouds in the sky. Every time I got too hetted up from peddlin' so fast, a cloud cooled me down. Then the sun would come back again like a promise of somethin' good ahead. And I seen so many flowers all over that day. Why, sometimes I thought this old world might not be such a bad place after all.

I looked at miles of crops—corn, wheat, and alfalfa—and I wondered what Father Jensen was gonna do now. Well, he beat me his last time. I was shed of him for good.

I thought about home, about Pa, Uncle Roy, and Aunt Minnie. Where was Henry and Walter and Paul? I just hoped somebody will be glad to see me when I get home.

I kept going north. I got to Minneapolis in the wee hours of the morning when it was still dark, and I stopped to rest on a bench just sittin' there at the side of the road. Then I asked directions to the highway that would take me west to Fairhaven, and I was on my way again. After sun-up, when traffic got a bit thick, I laid myself down in the ditch and dozed off a little. The weeds and grass was soft and I went right to sleep. When I got up my legs was pretty stiff and sore, but I knew I was gettin' close to home. I could feel it.

I reached Fairhaven Hill a couple hours past noon. I was home! I got offen my bicycle and just stood there lookin' around. The town was smaller than I remembered all these years. All of a sudden I felt scared. Real scared! What if there weren't nobody here anymore that knowed who I was. Then I remembered what Ma always said to me. "God loves you, Harold. Always remember that." I guess I had forgotten that long time ago. Well, if God loves me, maybe he'll help me like he helped all those people in the stories Ma told me. "God," I said right out loud, "please let there be somebody here who is glad to see me come home again."

An old lady come walkin' along and I stopped and told her who I was. She said my Pa passed on a couple years ago, and Uncle Roy and Aunt Minnie were gone too, but Pa's brother Earl come back from Pennsylvania and lives on the old Merrill place near where we used to live. Did I know where that was? I weren't sure, so she directed me north of town and where to turn, and all, so I started out even though I never knowed my Uncle Earl before. They won't know me, but maybe they'll be glad to see me anyways.

Wind was pickin' up now, makin' headway harder and slower. I was excited and nervous about being home and all, and then I saw this big, old oak tree right up ahead. I remembered that tree. It put a big lump in my throat and my chest just burned like it was on fire.

When I got closer to that old oak tree I saw a big, black dog sittin under the tree, and when he caught sight of me comin' down the road, he started barkin' and come a-runnin' to me real fast. It shook me up some, but I weren't gonna let no dog stop me now. I just kept peddlin' as fast as I could, and that there dog just turned around and ran on ahead of me, wagging his tail, and turned left just where I needed to turn, and he just led me right to the old Merrill place and right up to the door. When I stopped, he almost knocked me over, jumpin' up on me and lickin' my face and everything. I sure didn't have to be scared of him.

A lady come out the door wipin' her hands on her apron, and said, "Hello, there, young man. I see you found our wandering dog. He took off yesterday morning and we were worried he went off to die someplace. He's getting pretty old. Where'd you find him?"

I told her about the old oak tree, and told her who I was and where I comed from and by the time I had all that told, my Uncle Earl come out from the machine shed and I had to tell it all again. And all the while that old dog just kept runnin' around in circles and jumpin' up on me until I finally just had to tell him to git down offen me.

"Don't you know that dog, son?" Uncle Earl said. "He's Teddy. He was your puppy before they took you away. We took him in after your Pa died. I guess he knew you were coming home and went out to meet you."

I just cried like a baby while Teddy licked my face. I guess God does love me, just like Ma said. He sent Teddy to meet me cuz he remembered me and he was glad to see me.

CHAPTER TWENTY-FOUR

HE DIDN'T LEAVE US

I cried when I heard cousin Harold's story. I was so happy Dad didn't have to be in that orphanage. His childhood was hard enough as it was. It made him a little different. In later years when Daylight Savings Time was put into practice, Dad refused to participate. His watch was set at central time every summer when all the other clocks in the state were set one hour later.

Dad's answers to questions about his childhood were short and vague, if he answered at all. He flexed the muscle of his jaw, a warning that he was angry, or at least uncomfortable. Mom told us not to ask Dad about those things.

"Why did the county take Dad and the other children away from their mother?" I asked Mom.

"Well, I guess she didn't want them," Mom said. "Dad's uncle Marsh raised Dad and his older brother Harvey, and the younger boys were adopted out. Only Aunt Cora was raised by their mother."

I couldn't imagine a mother not wanting her children. How would that make you feel? I learned the answer to that when I overheard Dad tell Aunt Cora, "I will hate my mother until the day I die."

I learned later from Aunt Cora, that he had loved his mother very much. When Dad believed that she didn't want him anymore, the only way he could keep his heart from breaking into little pieces was to become angry—and to stay angry.

He carried that anger with him until he died at the age of sixty-five, never knowing the truth. After his death, I went searching and discovered that an unscrupulous judge had taken his mother's children from her illegally so he could sell the two youngest boys to a wealthy couple. She spent the rest of her life trying to find and reclaim her children.

Well into his adulthood, Dad's brother, Harvey, cried every time he talked about their childhood. Dad just ground his teeth, worked his jaw muscles, and stared straight ahead.

By the time I was in junior high, I had learned a little about psychology. My desire was to go to college and become a marriage counselor. I don't know why a marriage counselor—that was just my interest. So I asked myself, "How can a man hate his mother and find love in his heart for other women?"

Did Dad love Mom? I never saw any evidence of romantic love. Did he love me? I had no evidence of that either. He hardly ever talked to me. "Children are to be seen and not heard," he said. He never participated in any of our school functions. But he worked hard to put food on the table for us. And, although he may have sometimes wanted out of the responsibility of a wife and five children, he never left us. That was what he thought his mother had done to him.

When I was just starting school, Dad borrowed money to build us a house at Bagley, Minnesota. For some reason, he lost the house. A few years later he had the courage to start his own trucking business. That also failed. Did he use poor judgment? Were there special circumstances that caused him to lose his business? I don't know. But I do know Mom lost confidence in him, and he evidently—maybe consequently—lost confidence in himself. With only an eighth-grade education, what was left for him to do except hard labor?

After hearing Dad's comment about hating his mother, I went to bed that night asking my Father in Heaven to make my dad not hate his mother anymore.

What My Father Told Me

- The world is not round. It is flat.
- It isn't ladylike to whistle.
- Don't play cards on Sunday.
- Don't change your clock for Daylight Savings Time. The cows don't know it's an hour earlier.
- Don't mix with blacks. (He used the "n" word.)

What I Wish My Father Had Told Me

- That he loved me.
- That I was smart and pretty and loveable.
- That I could be somebody someday.
- That I was important.
- That he was proud of me.
- That he knew and loved God.

What I Wish I Had Told My Parents

- That I have a Father in Heaven who loves me.
- That I love my Father in Heaven.

But how could I tell them that, when I had nothing more to tell? It wasn't until I had two children and began attending church that some of my childhood questions were answered—that I began to know more about my Heavenly Father. The fact that I sustained such strong faith all those years is evidence of God's grace. It was He who kept my faith strong.

CHAPTER TWENTY-FIVE

I LIED AND LIED

It is said that we cannot escape our heritage, as the blood of our ancestors forms the person we are destined to become. That being the case, I can trace my good moral character, my creativity, and my wanderlust as inherent in my genes. I claim my middle-class stature and anything above *low income* as a step up from whence I came.

On my mother's side, I come from poor, hard working, uneducated, but honest and creative Scandinavian immigrants. Yet my German paternal great-great-grandmother's family had class and social standing. They were well-known and well respected community leaders in Springfield, Illinois, where Abraham Lincoln lived. In fact, my paternal great-great-grandfather, Daniel Daniels, did some carpentry work for Mr. Lincoln at one time. But that class and social standing was somewhat neutralized when their granddaughter, my grandmother Ella Ingram, married Elvey Duncan, an uneducated Kentucky hillbilly of Scotch and Irish descent.

So who am I and where do I belong in this world of opportunities and expectations? Both my mother and father appear to be victims of their heritage. My mother, uneducated and too weak to demand what she deserved. My father, ignorant and too angry at all authority figures to remain in any job for long. Am I like my mother? Am I like my father?

Although I loved my parents, I strive to be unlike both. Yet I frequently recognize them in my own thoughts and actions.

I was fourteen and wanted a summer job—needed a summer job was more like it. My parents couldn't afford to buy us school clothes and supplies. So a job was a necessity. I had looked older than my age for years, and people said I acted older, so it wasn't too difficult to make my new employer believe my lie when I said I was sixteen. Unfortunately, I never have been a good liar, and I gave myself away partway through that summer job. Fortunately, by that time I had proven myself, so I wasn't fired.

My employer was Mrs. Katz, a woman who lived close enough so I could walk to work every day. My job was to care for their two children, clean house, do shopping, cook, and generally do whatever she asked me to do. The job paid fifty cents an hour.

Mrs. Katz was a somewhat portly woman, with dark wavy hair, and I liked her, within the framework of employer/employee status. With only a small amount of exertion in the heat of that summer, perspiration beaded on her forehead and ran down the sides of her face. That surprised me. My face never perspired. I had never seen a woman's face perspire before.

She liked the way I cleaned, getting into the corners. (My mother was a stickler about that.) She was surprised at how well I could handle myself in the kitchen, and she was even more surprised when I offered to sew buttons on her son's shirt. She didn't know how to sew.

One day when I was making sandwiches for lunch I put one thin slice of lunchmeat in each sandwich, the way I would have done at home. "What kind of sandwich is this?" Mrs. Katz asked with disgust. "Put about three or four of those slices of meat in there," she told me.

I could hardly believe it. What extravagance! They must be rich to put so much meat in one sandwich. And not just for her, but for the children and me as well.

One day when I was cleaning cupboards and she was in the kitchen talking with me, she asked me where our family goes on vacations. "We don't go on vacations," I told her.

"You've never been on a vacation?" she asked. "What does your father do with his time off from his job?"

"He doesn't get any time off," I told her.

"Everyone gets vacation time from his or her job," she insisted. "Where does he work?"

At that time my dad hadn't been at his present job very long. His jobs were always manual labor jobs. He was a hothead who would get mad at his boss about something and quit his job on the spot. Often it meant that he would come home and tell Mom, "We're moving, so get packed."

When Mrs. Katz held up that mirror to our family, I could see that our family was not *normal*. That gave me many hours of contemplation. If my father had stayed at one job for a reasonable amount of time, he could have had a paid vacation. We might have taken a trip somewhere—seen another part of the country—had time together as a family. As it was, I hardly ever saw my father. It would have been nice to have a vacation.

And how did my mother feel about never having a vacation? Mom was working at Fanny Farmer Candy Company in Minneapolis at that time. Her days were long and hard too. When she came home from work she had more work to do, just as did my dad. Did she even know that most people had vacations? It seemed as if our family and all our relatives and friends did the same things we did. I don't recall anyone that I knew, other than Mrs. Katz, taking a vacation while I was growing up. They were farmers and manual laborers who never had enough money for their needs, let alone meeting any of the wants in their lives.

I never asked Mom or Dad about vacations. It didn't seem like the thing to do.

I was still fourteen when we moved to a house in an alley in North Minneapolis. The address had ½ in it. Mom worked at White Way Cleaners, and one day when she was gone I had some friends over and made brownies as a treat for them. Mom was angry with me when she got home. "We can't afford to feed the neighbor kids," she said.

Mom wanted to move later because black people had moved in next door. I had never been ashamed of my mother before, but I was ashamed of her then. A neighbor lady told Mom about Mr. and Mrs. McEachern's house for rent. So we moved again.

I was fourteen when we moved to the upstairs of that house on Third Avenue, one block north of Plymouth Avenue and one block west of Washington Avenue—one block shy each way of the "bad neighborhood." It had two bedrooms, kitchen, bath, and back porch. We four girls slept in one bedroom, in two double beds, and Lee slept on the couch in the living room.

When school started in the fall, I worked after school and on Saturdays with my brother bussing dishes at the Hampshire Arms Hotel dining room on Fourth Avenue. The hotel was old and had been made into permanent apartments. The people who lived there and ate in the dining room treated Lee and me like disrespected servants. One old woman deliberately dropped her napkin on the floor and called me over to pick it up. "Well, put it on my lap," she ordered when I tried to hand it to her. Then she dismissed me with such disdain I felt as if I had been slapped.

As we walked home together, Lee and I compared notes on how badly the residents treated us. He hated it there as much as

I did. One day I had taken enough guff and I quit. *Am I like my father?* It certainly made me understand him a little better and I cut him some slack.

After I quit my job at the Hampshire Arms, I got a job at a bakery on Broadway. I loved working there on Saturdays and after school, waiting on customers who were usually nice, putting fresh, fragrant loaves of bread through the automatic slicer and then sliding the sliced loaf into a bag. *That took skill, you know.* I loved making change. I just loved it all.

And I loved Doris, one of the girls who worked there. She was older than I, of course. I had lied about my age again. I didn't like lying, but I needed the job and they wouldn't have hired me at my real age. I told my Heavenly Father that I was sorry for lying, but I think He understood it was necessary, because I never felt too bad about it. Anyway, I knew that He forgave me when I said I was sorry.

Doris had long, dark hair that was even beautiful and shiny under a hairnet. She had huge blue eyes that were always happy, and she was so much fun.

I had never met anyone with such a playful spirit. And she was funny. We laughed a lot when we worked together. Laughter was not a part of my life and she made me realize how wonderful laughter feels. I found myself wanting to go to work more to see her than anything else. She wore cologne that to this day I think about Doris if I smell that scent.

I went to see the movie *Picnic,* starring Kim Novak and William Holden. Never before had a movie had such an effect on me. As William Holden awakened the libido of Kim Novak in the movie, he also awakened mine. When he danced that slow dance with Kim, I melted. The song "Moon Glow" was a favorite of mine for many years, bringing back the powerful emotions that romantic music and sensuous dance evokes.

I always enjoyed reading, and during that time in my life I read the book, *My Love Affair with the State of Maine,* written by Scotty Mackenzie and Ruth Goode. Two young women leave their New York jobs and move to Maine where they decide to open a shop. I fell in love with everything about Maine and decided I want to visit Maine some day. I still have not been to Maine, but I plan to change that very soon.

That fall Dad was working for Kliers Nursery and Garden Center in Minneapolis. McEachern's sold the house we were renting, so we moved to an upstairs apartment at Dupont and Franklin Avenue. Now we were in the "bad neighborhood." This was a dingy apartment above a grocery store where we shared a toilet down the hall with several other families. We had no bathing facilities other than the galvanized tub we used once a week in our kitchen. Since I was the oldest girl I always got to bathe first, thankfully. Then my three sisters bathed according to age and finally it was Lee's turn. Poor guy! The water would be pretty cruddy by the time he got into that tub. Not that he could really get into it, as it was too small. But he could stand in it, crouch and wash. He was already sixteen years old. I was fourteen.

In that apartment over the grocery store, Mom's old treadle sewing machine sat in the back porch area where the light was good. That's where I did a lot of sewing. Because people knew how poor we were, many gave us the clothes they no longer wanted. I learned to sew by taking those clothes apart and altering them for use by our family. I also learned to make new clothes out of old clothes—slacks from an old coat, a small dress from a large dress, a blouse from a dress, and so forth.

One of the dresses we got from someone was absolutely beautiful! It was black brocade with gold embroidered flowers overall. It was much too large for me, but I altered it to fit and was glad I had that dress when I had occasion for it. The occasion was John Ross.

The Frank Ross family was one of the other families living above the grocery store down the hall from us. Frank worked a rubbish route, and he got Dad a job working there too. The Ross's had eight children, the oldest being John, a soldier whom I hadn't met until he came home on leave. He was drop-dead gorgeous! And he liked me.

John had been stationed in France. He asked me out on a date, but I already had a date with someone else that evening. He said, "When you get home from your date I'll be waiting for you. Just come to the end of the hallway."

I could hardly wait for my movie date to end so I could see John Ross. Of course, I had worn my beautiful newly-renovated black embroidered dress. I said good night to my date at the door and waited until I knew he was down the stairs. Then I walked around the corner and to the end of the hall.

Our hallway was not the brightly painted, well-lit, carpeted hallway of today's apartment buildings. The walls were dark brown wood, the floor was dark brown wood, and it was dark in the halls. But when I arrived at the little alcove at the end of the hallway, John Ross was waiting for me.

He had laid quilts on the floor so we could sit, and propped sofa pillows against the wall so we could lean back comfortably. Lit candles cast a romantic glow over the corner, and classical music playing softly on a portable record player set the mood. John complimented me on my dress and told me that French girls wear black nylon stockings. "Black stockings would look great with that dress," he told me.

I had never seen American women wearing black stockings. I looked at my flesh-colored stockings and could not, for the life of me, envision wearing black nylon stockings. That should probably have been the first clue that I would never be a fashion plate, although I do now wear black stockings with a black dress.

While we slowly sipped wine—one glass only—and kissed occasionally as we cuddled, we listened to Rachmaninoff's *Piano Concerto #2 in C Minor*, a piece of music I still listen to with nostalgia for that most romantic, but innocent, evening with a handsome young man in uniform.

CHAPTER TWENTY-SIX
ONLY A CHILD

The steps we take that move us forward toward adulthood are the moments most remembered. They are often painful, or they strike a chord within us that reverberates like a bong—a recognition or understanding, a life lesson learned. We know we are grown up. Our childhood is behind us. Some reach that stage at a relatively young age, and others take longer.

The following summer I turned fifteen. I worked at the YWCA cafeteria at Twelfth and Nicollet in downtown Minneapolis. Of course, I was supposed to be sixteen, but once again I had lied. Dressing in my white uniform made me feel so professional. I made salads and kept the display case filled as customers came by and made their selections.

Before the end of the summer my boss put me in charge of the salad section. One day while I was shredding cabbage I sliced the end of my thumb off into the cabbage. By the time my thumb had been bandaged, I discovered that someone else had continued to make the coleslaw, thumb flesh and all. Yuk!! I have often thought about that and felt badly that someone possibly ate that tiny piece of flesh.

One of the nicest things about that job was the long walk to downtown and back every day. My good friend, Corrina Torres, worked with me, and we walked to work together every day, rain or shine, laughing and talking, as good friends do. She was a gorgeous, flamboyant, Hispanic girl whose beauty I envied. Lee had a crush on her.

We walked from my home at Plymouth and Third Street to Twelfth and Nicollet—a good long walk. We walked south on Fourth Street until we came to the railroad bridge—the Seventh Street Bridge, as it was called—the entrance into downtown. It was a two-lane highway with a walkway on each side. As we reached the top of the bridge and the skyline of downtown came into view, I felt that familiar catch in my throat and became exhilarated with a sense of freedom and just being alive.

We stopped at the rise of the bridge, leaned over the hard, metal rail and waved hello to the handful of men working below the bridge. They waved, yelled hello, and sometimes gave us long, low, wolf whistles. The tingle of pure excitement in the pit of my stomach never failed to appear. I loved the downtown energy. The people, the hustle and bustle, the life.

I felt so free on that bridge, so on the brink of an exciting life, going into the heart of the big city with all the mystery that had not yet been revealed. It wasn't until years later that I realized that bridge was my transition point in life. On that bridge, the gateway to the city, I changed from dependent to independent, from poor to earning an income, from girl to young woman, and from the present to the future.

My boyfriend at the time was Arthur. He was seventeen. Because of my work schedule at the YWCA cafeteria, I always had time between lunch and dinner for myself. Art met me and we spent time at Loring Park feeding the squirrels or at Schmidt's Music Store where we listened to music. He introduced me to classical music, something about which, up until that time, I knew nothing. That fall Art asked me to go to the state fair with him. I had never been to the state fair and was looking forward to a fun day. Mom said, "No."

"Why not?" I asked her.

"Because I said so." That was her pat answer any time she said no to a request. So I didn't get to go to the state fair with a nice young man that year. I decided that I would never tell my children, "Because I said so."

When we went back to school that fall I met Pia, a stunningly beautiful student who was in my class. Years later I often wondered if Loni Anderson, the movie actress, wasn't really the Pia from North High that I knew. Pia was that beautiful, that full-figured, that stunning, and Pia looked like Loni Anderson. Art looked at her!! That made me insanely jealous. How could he find me attractive after looking at Pia? Pia and I never became friends, and I think she left North High before I did.

One night when I was out with Art we were parked in the car listening to the radio, talking, and kissing. Of course I never allowed inappropriate touching, but we got a lot of mileage out of just kissing each other. Art was fun to talk with as well. So we talked and kissed and listened to music. All of a sudden Art said, "Wake up, we've been sleeping. It's late." We had both fallen asleep.

It was way past my curfew and I worried all the way home what my mother would say. When we got home, Art walked me to the door and Mom met us there. "You're late," she said.

"It was Connie's fault," Art said. "She didn't want to come home yet."

I couldn't believe my ears! *How could he lie like that? And how could he blame me?* I refused to see him anymore. I no longer respected him. He tried to explain that he thought my mother wouldn't make me stop seeing him if she thought I had been to blame. It didn't matter. I never dated him again.

What I wanted most that summer of 1957 was a camera. I saved my earnings from the YWCA and bought a Brownie Hawkeye camera with flash attachment. Ironically, that same day my dad came home with our first television set—a large brown box with the screen set in the top half. When I got home Dad was on the floor installing this new-fangled electronic machine. I saw a photo opportunity, brought my new camera into the living room, and snapped Dad's picture.

Poor Dad! When the flashbulb went off he thought something had exploded in the television. My exciting news about having a new camera wasn't met with the enthusiasm I had hoped for.

I saw another good photo opportunity shortly after that when my mother came home with a set of false teeth. She had the teeth in her hands and was showing them to Dad when I directed the camera toward her and snapped the picture. Off went the flashbulb, bright enough to temporarily blind a person. Once again, my parents were less than pleased to have a photo-happy daughter in the household.

Our new television proved to be a wonderful source of entertainment for our whole family as all seven of us crowded on and around the sofa to watch *The Jackie Gleason Show*, *The Ed Sullivan Show*, *Make Room for Daddy*, and *The Loretta Young Show*. Dad and Lee watched wrestling. When we came home from school, we watched *The Mickey Mouse Club*. Annette Funicello was my favorite Mouseketeer.

My mother's father, John Abraham Pajari, was killed in a car accident August 2, 1957. He was seventy-four. It happened on Highway 71 between Menahga and Park Rapids at what local people refer to as three mile corner where Grandpa would have turned off to come home. His old Model T Ford was so smashed that he couldn't possibly have survived. Both people in the other car died as well.

Grandpa was buried at Green Valley Cemetery in the country, not far from their farm. His two sons Fred and Arlie were already laid to rest there in the family plot that Grandpa had purchased. I felt sad that Grandpa was gone, but I realized that he had had a good long life. I felt bad for Grandma, who was left without a husband. But her grown sons, Harvey and Richard, still lived with her, so I knew she wouldn't be alone. Mom seemed to be doing okay.

I was surprised at my own lack of sympathy in that situation. I thought I should be heartbroken and crying and grieving for months. I wasn't. I wondered whether I was an uncaring person. It was much later that I learned Grandpa had only had one beer at the bar before he left for home that day, and no one knew the cause of the accident.

That summer I frequently took my three little sisters downtown. We took a bus to Marquette Avenue where our first stop was the Foshay Tower, the tallest building in Minneapolis. We rode the elevator to the thirty-first floor observation deck and looked across the city where we "could see for thirty miles on a clear day," according to the brochure. Then we visited the Minneapolis library on Hennepin Avenue, where we went immediately to the third floor museum to see the Egyptian mummy from 3000 BC. It never stopped giving my sisters a thrill to see a real mummy all wrapped in gauze.

Later we went to Seventh and Hennepin to the Nankin Café and had a Chinese lunch. We might do some window shopping at Dayton's department store before we stopped at the beauty shop on Seventh Street where Aunt Alice worked, just to say hello. She always made a big deal about her "beautiful" nieces as she introduced us to all her clients and co-workers.

Sometimes I took my sisters to movies, or concerts, or plays, or festivals, or fairs. I wanted them to be exposed to things that my parents didn't expose me to. I was fortunate to have friends who taught me things that my parents couldn't teach me.

I was already dating in junior high, but I always made time for my sisters. By the time I was in senior high, I became so busy with working and dating that I no longer took my sisters to as many places. By then, they too were busy with school and friends.

I became so busy with my life that I rarely thought about my Heavenly Father, although I always acted in a way that I believed He wanted me to act, even apologizing to Him when I lied about my age. I tried to follow the Ten Commandments I had learned about at confirmation classes. I honored my parents. I didn't steal. I tried to love all people. I didn't swear. My parents worked on Sunday, however, and I worked on Sunday. We never attended church services. We didn't even own a Bible.

Today I wonder why, when I loved my Heavenly Father so much, and I never lost faith in Him, didn't I seek answers to the many questions I had about Him? Why didn't I go to church on my own if my family didn't want to go? Why didn't I buy a Bible?

I like to think that I grew up early—that I was mature at fifteen and sixteen years of age. Yet I was immature in many ways. Although I was assertive in going after jobs that I wanted—that was out of dire need—I certainly was not assertive in other ways. I never set goals. I had never heard of that concept. The only dream I ever had was to go to college and become a marriage counselor, and I allowed my mother to dash that dream by telling me that they couldn't afford to send me to college.

At school I never discussed future education with teachers or counselors. I never got into trouble, so I never came to anyone's attention. I didn't even know I might have been able to discuss my desires with someone at school. With my good grades, and my parents' low income, I could have probably gotten scholarships, had I known about the possibility.

I had no one to model the behavior of an educated person or a Christian. How was I to know better?

I was not grown up. I was still just a child.

CHAPTER TWENTY-SEVEN

HIGH SCHOOL YEARS

I attended North High School for my sophomore and junior years, always working in the school office to pay for my lunches, and working part-time at other jobs during the evenings and weekends. Most of the time, I found school boring. I hated the mandatory gym classes, believing that girls shouldn't play football. That was for boys. I wasn't good at basketball either. Or tennis. And I sure couldn't climb a rope!

While I failed miserably at sports, I otherwise learned easily. But I stayed home a lot to help Mom when I knew what we were going to be doing in classes that day wasn't important. Still, I maintained a "B" average except for my typing class. One cannot learn a manual skill unless one practices. I didn't have a typewriter at home, so I got a "D" in typing. How humiliating for an honor student!

I still did the grocery shopping and much of the cooking. Our standard fare was hamburger patties made with enough oatmeal and cracker fillers so one pound of meat would feed seven people. Cooked potatoes and gravy, a can of vegetables, and home made biscuits rounded out the evening meal. I made the gravy with potato and vegetable water so as to retain as many vitamins as possible. Potatoes and biscuits made up the major part of our dinners, with only a small hamburger and a small serving of vegetables to round it out. Sometimes I made macaroni hot dish using the standard one-pound of ground beef, macaroni, and a can of tomato soup. Lunches were often canned soup or grilled cheese sandwiches. Breakfast was cooked oatmeal or Cream of Wheat or fried eggs with toast. No gourmet cooks at our house.

But after their financial situation improved, Mom made wonderful Christmas cookies. She packed them in empty oatmeal boxes, wrapped them in pretty paper, and gave them to special people at Christmas, such as our teachers and the mailman. She also made wonderful dill pickles, flatbread, and strawberry-rhubarb jelly.

My best friends in high school were Carolyn Bach and Marge Otte, but I had little time to spend with them. I never attended football games or any of the school activities because I always had a job to go to immediately after school.

My income went to buy school clothes and supplies, bus fares, gifts, cosmetics, and personal hygiene items. I opened a Christmas account at the bank and deposited money each week for Christmas gifts.

Learning from my parents the ramifications of not having money when needs arise, I began to budget money instead of spending everything as soon as I got it. I also learned a lesson from my sister Judie, whom we called "moneybags" because she always had money stashed away.

One day when my parents were not home, a salesman came to the house selling lamps that looked like flowers made of glass petals, with a small bulb in the center. They were beautiful, and both Judie and I wanted to buy one. Judie dug out her money and paid for her lamp. I didn't have enough money. But the nice salesman told me that he would give me the lamp today and I could make payments on it. Well, when I finished making all the payments, I realized how much more my lamp had cost than what Judie had paid for hers. It was a good lesson I have never forgotten about the cost of doing things by credit.

I also learned to be thrifty by making many of my own clothes. It wasn't always enough to meet my needs, but it helped.

I was invited to the junior prom but refused the invitation because I didn't have enough money saved to buy a dress and shoes. Mom said they couldn't afford to help me out. I had just bought my winter coat, hat, and mittens, and that had taken the rest of the money I had saved.

We had an early snowfall that winter, and I hadn't saved enough money to buy winter snow boots yet. I was walking to school through the deep snow in shoes and stockings and met a man on the sidewalk who looked at my wet feet with disgust. He practically spat at me. I knew he was thinking I was just a stupid girl, too vain to wear decent footwear in this weather. I was miserable and cold, and that man's dirty look almost made me cry.

Earlier that year I had bought a pattern, wool fabric, and thread to make a suit for myself. While I paid for a purchase at another store, with my shopping bag near my feet, someone stole my bag with the fabric in it. There went my hard-earned money. It was weeks before I could afford to buy more fabric for the suit I wanted. However when I did, that suit I made was one of the most wonderful outfits I ever owned. It was good-quality turquoise wool. I lined it and tailored it with bound buttonholes and expensive, classy buttons. It fit well, looked great, and I felt good whenever I wore it. I wish I still fit into it.

During our high school years we spent quite a bit of time with our Uncle Harvey's family. One day we went to Osseo with our cousin Janet and her boyfriend Reuben to watch Pretty Boy Larry Hennig wrestle. It was at an outdoor arena and we were standing ringside—so close, in fact, that Janet reached into the ring and grabbed the toe of Larry's opponent and twisted it. I was shocked. But that was Janet—daring to risk doing things I was too inhibited to do. Like my mother, if it was beyond total safety or not socially "nice," I didn't do it.

Like driving on a frozen lake. Lee Anderson drove out on a lake once when we were together. He was sliding in circles and having a wonderful time. I was terrified! I was afraid we would crack the ice open and fall in.

Lee Anderson was my brother's good friend, and I had known him for many years. I began dating him when I was barely sixteen. Lee was nice looking but not particularly handsome. He had light brown hair and full lips. After we started dating I loved kissing him. Sometimes our necking session got pretty heated up—more than with any other boyfriend. Many times, I do believe my Heavenly Father was in control, because I almost was not.

In 1957 we were invited to my cousin Ruthie's wedding. I was almost sixteen and it would be the first wedding I had ever attended. I made my dress; then I made dresses for Donna, Judie, and Irene. We all looked good as we drove to the wedding—Dad in a suit and Mom pretty in a new dress she bought for the occasion.

The wedding was held at St. Stephen's Catholic Church. Ruthie was beautiful in a long, white wedding dress and veil, and her maid of honor wore a tea length blue dress. The groom and his twin brother were in light gray suits. The service was nice, and the music beautiful, and the vows made me cry. Then we went to her parent's home in north Minneapolis for the reception. Ruthie tossed the bouquet and Donna caught it. They had a grand array of food in the dining room and a beautiful multi-layered wedding cake. We were all in the back yard of their modest home at 818 Russell Avenue North when we heard screaming from the front yard. As we rushed to the front, a car squealed away. Irene was running from the street to the house, still screaming.

Irene, who was nine, told us she had been playing in the front yard and a man stopped his car and came over to her. "If you could have anything you want," he said. "What would it be?"

"Roller skates," Irene said.

"Okay, let's go get you some roller skates," he said.

Irene started toward the car but said, "Wait, I have to go tell Mom. I'll be right back." The man grabbed her arm and tried to force her into the car. Of course, Irene got scared and began screaming. When he saw people coming to her aid, he fled.

With Irene's description of the man, several of the wedding guests said they had seen him and spoken to him, but none of them knew him. Mom praised Irene profusely for being smart enough to scream and fight.

We came that close to losing our youngest sister. If that man had been successful in getting her in the car, we would have probably never seen Irene again. I don't think Mom could have survived that tragedy.

CHAPTER TWENTY-EIGHT

PROBLEMS

After I finished my junior year at North High, Dad moved us to south Minneapolis, near the First Augustana Lutheran Church. We lived on the second floor of a home at 1505 South Tenth Avenue, owned by Mr. and Mrs. Konopliv. This was a giant step up from our former address above the grocery store.

This boxy two-story house looked almost stately. The neighborhood was clean and quiet, and Elliot Park was only half a block away. A wide, polished, wooden staircase drew us to the second level where the floors were hardwood, the dining room included a built-in buffet with glass doors, and square pillars separated the dining room from the living room. Large windows cast sunny rays of light across the floors, and a cozy back porch was enclosed with both screens and windows. I shared a bedroom with only one sister, two other sisters shared the third bedroom, and Lee slept on the couch. Poor Lee! He always got the short end of the stick. But he never complained.

Here we had a private bathroom for our own family. The kitchen was small, but we had a large dining room for our family to eat together.

Mom took a job at Treasure Masters. She walked to and from work, cutting across Elliot Park. Mom and Dad were not getting along at that time. I often heard them arguing in their bedroom, trying to talk quietly so we wouldn't hear them. "You could have picked me up from work," Mom said one evening. "You weren't home all day, like you said. The hood of the car was warm when I got home. Were you with Emily?"

Emily was a neighbor whose daughter Irene often babysat. A single mother, Emily was outgoing, assertive, and passionate. She had full breasts, thick, dark, rich, auburn hair ("like a strawberry roan," Dad said. He loved horses). Emily had a deep, throaty voice, and she laughed a lot. I could see that Mom looked meek and mousey in comparison.

I felt disgusted seeing Dad change when Emily came over. He took on a charming, flirty persona. His face softened. The crinkles by his eyes deepened. So did his voice. He couldn't seem to stop looking at her. I wanted to yell at Dad, "What are you thinking?" But I knew what he was thinking, and it made me disgusted with him.

Changes took place in Mom too when Emily was at our house. While Mom had liked Emily when she first met her, the friendship that might have bloomed between them was quickly squelched when Dad's attraction to her became so obvious. Mom became stiff and cold to her, and soon she stopped coming over—at least when Mom was home. I prayed that everything would be okay between Mom and Dad.

One night they were arguing in their bedroom again (as if we couldn't hear them), and Mom told Dad, "Go then! Go live with your hussy, if that's what you want!"

Dad didn't leave, and a few days later he was under the car doing some repairs and the jack slipped. The car fell on his face, crushing one cheek and his jaw. Fortunately, he wasn't hurt worse than that. His jaw was wired closed for months. Dad took all his nourishment through a straw, and Mom was a good caregiver, as far as I could see.

Dad was never as handsome after that. The affair with Emily was evidently over.

⁂

I was sixteen, and immediately after we moved, I got a job working at the Dairy Queen a couple blocks away. This time I didn't have to lie about my age. The Dairy Queen was a small building with only a walk-up window for ordering. We only served ice milk products, and it was all takeout. I worked unsupervised and alone.

My boss, an older man who came in daily to pour mix into the machine and collect the money, learned that I had never tasted pizza. One night after we closed, he invited me out for pizza. "The Pizzeria on Lake Street has the best pizza anywhere," he told me. "You have to have some."

I agreed to go have pizza with him, assuming it was an innocent meal shared by two people who knew each other. The pizza was wonderful, but afterward, my boss wanted payment for the dinner he had just bought me. I had a long and difficult struggle with him in the car parked behind the Dairy Queen before he finally let me out.

He didn't fire me, and I didn't quit, but I stayed cool to him after that. He was hardly ever there anyway. I opened the shop and managed it by myself. He never made another pass at me.

Were all men sex-crazy? I wondered. Do I have to be careful of men? "Keep me safe," I whispered to the Father I always relied upon.

⁂

One day I was off work, and Mom and I had spent the better part of the day washing clothes and hanging them out on the clotheslines. Mom was a fastidious laundress, making certain that the whites were sparkling white and the rest of the clothes just as clean. She had a method of hanging them just right on the lines too. All like clothes must be hung together. I was always proud of looking at our laundry on the lines. They flapped in the breeze, and dried in the sun, and came into the house smelling like fresh air.

Late that afternoon Mom went outside to get the clothes from the line. She came in empty-handed, wearing a face as white as her laundry. "Someone stole our clothes," she announced. I couldn't believe it. But someone had, in fact, taken all our laundry.

This was a tragedy for a family of seven that had few clothes to begin with and less money to buy more. We had no sheets to put on the beds that night, no towels, and hardly any clothes to wear. It is still hard to believe that someone would stoop low enough to steal the clothes right off our clotheslines in broad daylight. But that is what they did.

CHAPTER TWENTY-NINE

ENGAGED

A young man who worked at the Clark service station on the corner near the Dairy Queen came frequently to buy a cone. He had eager blue eyes, an honest smile, broad shoulders, and narrow hips. The virility of his youth was resplendent with every flex of his muscles as he ran from the Clark station to the Dairy Queen, and then back again. As he ordered his usual cone, his eyes expressed an interest in me his tongue couldn't seem to verbalize.

One day I ran out of mix in the machine, and the cans were too heavy for me to lift. "Go to the Clark station and ask the young man working there to come and help me," I said to a girl who was hanging around. In only a couple minutes the guy came running from the Clark station. "How can I help you?" he asked me.

I would later learn that David Lounsbury grew up on a farm, was twenty-three and had served three years in the Army. He worked as a surgical orderly at St. Barnabas Hospital, and worked the Clark Station as his second job. He was saving money to buy a farm.

Our first date was in May 1958, about three weeks before I turned seventeen. We went to a drive-in movie. David was polite and considerate. He went into the concession stand and bought popcorn and sodas. After we finished eating the popcorn, he put his arm around me and pulled me closer to him. He walked me to the door when we said goodnight and didn't try to kiss me, but we made a date for the next day to go to the beach.

We went to Cedar Lake beach, swam, lay in the sun and talked. It was a nice, relaxing day and we got better acquainted. In spite of working two jobs, David found at least a little time each day to see me. We went to drive-in movies, drive-in restaurants, and to the beach. If we went to the beach during the day, David always invited my three sisters to go with us. They adored David.

I felt as if I had known David forever. He was open and honest, hardworking, shared my values, and was ambitious and affectionate. My parents liked him.

David kissed me after our second date. We did a lot of kissing on succeeding dates, but I always put the brakes on before we went too far. But David and I were falling in love, and I wanted more and more of him each day. Most of the time we were comfortable with each other just sitting in the car, listening to the radio, talking, and watching the weather ball atop the Northwestern National Bank Building glowing red. It would be warmer tomorrow.

I went up north to visit my grandparents for the Fourth of July weekend with my parents. It was the longest weekend of my life. I missed David so much. He was all I could think about. We got home the evening of the sixth, and David called shortly after I returned. I would never have called him, of course. Nice girls didn't call boys back then.

David picked me up in his snazzy, brand new, black and silver '57 Chevrolet Bel Air. We drove for a while, his arm around me, telling me he had missed me as much as I had missed him. Finally he parked the car beneath some trees at Calhoun Beach and wound both arms around me with a kiss. It was dark by then.

After we kissed each other for a while, David let go of me, reached into the glove compartment of the car and took out a small box. He opened it, showed me an engagement ring inside, and said, "Will you marry me?"

My heart burst into shivers that radiated through my whole body. I hadn't expected anything like that. We had only been dating for a few weeks—less than two months—actually. I was barely seventeen. David would be twenty-four soon. I guess he felt old enough, but I had my senior year of high school yet.

"Yes, I'll marry you, David." I was shimmering with love, romance, and the excitement of being engaged.

David took the ring out of the velvet slot in the box and slid it on my finger. "With all my love forever, darling," he said. When he kissed me, I thought that life was never going to get any better than this. David was everything I could ever want in a husband. I knew he would always be faithful. I knew he would always care for me and support me, and that he would be a good father.

"I have a year of high school left, you know," I told him.

"Why do you need to finish high school?" he asked. "You'll never need to work after we're married. I'll take care of you."

"Well, can't we be engaged for a year and get married after I graduate?"

"I can't wait that long. Let's get married soon."

I knew he was thinking of sex. I too found it hard to stop when we were in the throes of a heavy make out session. But Mom had always told me that no decent guy would marry me if I weren't a virgin. So I always put on the brakes, and David had always honored my wishes in that regard, even though I often felt guilty letting things get so heated up and then pushing him away. I didn't want to stop either, but I didn't dare ruin my chances of getting a *decent* husband.

I had long wanted to go to college and become a marriage counselor. "College is for rich kids," my mother had told me when I had expressed that wish to her. "We can't afford to send you to college. You'll just have to do what we all do: get married and have children."

Now David was telling me I didn't need to finish high school. I knew I couldn't go to college. Maybe he was right. Maybe I didn't need to finish high school either. I told David I would think about it, as I closely examined my beautiful new diamond engagement ring, perfect in its one-quarter-carat solitaire diamond flanked by flowers carved into white gold, set in a yellow gold band. It fit me perfectly.

Though my parents totally approved of David, they seemed concerned about my age when we announced our engagement. I said we hadn't decided yet when we would get married. That satisfied them for the time being.

The next time David and I went out, we went to a movie. Afterward David parked behind the house where he lived in a rented room. It was dark and secluded in the yard, and we had never gone there before. After a few minutes of kissing, David unbuttoned my blouse. That was going further than I had let him go before. It was *really* hard to put the brakes on that night. But I did, and it served to make my decision. We would be married in October. I would not go back to school in September. After all, I wouldn't have to work after we were married. I would be a wife and a mother. All mothers stayed home with their children.

We planned a weekend trip to Paynesville to announce our engagement and so I could meet David's parents. During most of the ninety-minute drive on Friday evening, I grilled David on family names. His parents were Russell and Carol Lounsbury. They had thirteen children, but Dorothy died in childhood from a bee sting. It would be a challenge to remember their names and who belonged to whom.

David's parents were nice and seemed to approve of me. They had retired from the farm and lived in a modest home nearby. His father remained active traveling to dairy farms to test the quality and quantity of their cow's milk production for Dairy Herd

Improvement Association. It appeared David's mom was going out of her way to cook elaborately on my account.

I met all his siblings who lived in that area and, as I suspected, it was difficult to remember everyone's name, and especially who was married to whom. They were all likeable and seemed like good people. By the time we drove home after meeting David's family, I felt even better about marrying David.

CHAPTER THIRTY

THE THINGS I DIDN'T KNOW

I washed my face, applied a soft pink lipstick, and brushed my dishwater blonde hair into a soft pageboy style. Next I put on my turquoise uniform, beige nylon stockings, and white shoes. I hadn't started wearing other makeup yet, being blessed with smooth, blemish-free skin. I picked up my purse, said goodbye to Mom, and began my fifteen-minute walk to work. I was barely seventeen, but I had lied about my age, again, to get a job at St. Barnabas Hospital in Minneapolis as a nurse's aide. The qualifying age for this job was eighteen.

It was August, and my nylon uniform made a slick sound whenever my arm brushed my side. It served as a reminder that I was going to an important job, a job of an adult, a job to care for others. I took patients' pulses and temperatures, fed patients unable to feed themselves, gave bed baths, changed bedding, brought bedpans to patients, gave back rubs, cleaned patients who were incontinent, and generally did menial work. I enjoyed my work and the camaraderie with nurses and doctors when we all sat down at "report" and discussed patients and their cases. I felt good as I walked across Elliot Park to the hospital.

I was slim, healthy, and glowing with the full bloom of youth. I was an average-looking, normal young woman who rarely considered how I looked, other than to wonder whether I should wear my hair down or in a ponytail. I was five feet six and a half inches tall with a twenty-three-inch waistline. I weighed 118 pounds.

How I wish I could go back to that young girl and say, "Give thanks for your youthful face and body. Pay attention to yourself. Remember how you looked, because you will not always look this way." But of course I can't do that, so I just look at her picture on occasion in amazement that she didn't know how beautifully the bloom of youth sat upon her.

Perhaps, if she had known, it would have given her confidence to look beyond what her parents told her was possible for her life. She might have asked someone else if it were true that she couldn't go to college because her parents didn't have the money. Perhaps she might have met someone who told her girls do have an option other than getting married and having children. Maybe someone would have told her David was wrong when he said she didn't have to finish high school because she would never have to work after they got married.

Would she have had the confidence to seek out someone with whom she could discuss her Heavenly Father? Or was she so much like her quiet, introverted mother that it wouldn't have made a difference?

If her mother's preoccupation with being poor had not become so ingrained in her young mind, might she have worked at fewer jobs, thus giving herself more time to read? Maybe she would have learned more about the world around her, instead of remaining in her mother's small world.

I was so young and naïve. My ignorance was a source of embarrassment for me on several occasions at that hospital job. The first embarrassment came was when I was caring for a middle-aged man. Since he had suffered a heart attack, he was not allowed to do anything for himself for quite a long time. He wasn't even allowed to feed himself. That was my job.

On this particular morning his breakfast tray included a cooked egg served in an eggcup. I had never seen an eggcup and I didn't know how to open the egg. We never had cooked eggs at our house. For more than sixteen years I had eaten only fried eggs. So I put the egg on the plate and tried to cut it with a knife. It worked, but it was a soft-cooked egg and the yolk ran all over the plate.

The patient, frustrated with his inability to do things for himself, became irate. "Don't you know how to serve a cooked egg?" he yelled. "You're supposed to keep it in the egg cup."

Well, no, I didn't know how to serve a cooked egg. That was one more thing other people knew that I didn't know. At that moment I was angry with my mother. Why hadn't she taught me about eggcups and cooked eggs? What was wrong with my family that we didn't do things the way other people did them?

I picked up the patient's tray, saying, "I'll get you a new tray," and I left the room before he could see my tears of embarrassment. I swallowed my pride and asked another nurse's aide how to serve an egg in an eggcup. Later my mother said she had never heard of an eggcup.

Another time I was embarrassed because of my ignorance of worldly things was when a particularly handsome younger man was my patient. One day he told me, "You can put your shoes under my bed anytime, honey."

"What do you mean?" I asked him, thinking that my shoes were partly under his bed as I gave him his back rub. Did he like the back rubs I gave him better than those from other aides? "I mean, when I get out of here," he said. "You can put your shoes under my bed anytime."

Then, thinking I might have gotten the drift of understanding, I didn't know what to say. So I didn't respond at all. Later I told David what the patient had said to me, and David explained what he meant. The next day I was embarrassed when I saw that patient again, and when the patient once again made a suggestive remark to me, I walked out and told my head nurse. She assigned an older, large, gruff nurse's aide to care for him. I was angry that I couldn't handle him myself, but I just didn't know what to say to him. I was seventeen already. I was engaged to be married. Why couldn't I handle a pass from another man?

I felt totally grown up, but I didn't have a driver's license. I asked Dad if he would teach me to drive. He said he would, but he didn't find time, so David began to give me driving lessons. It scared me to drive his brand new car, but he assured me that nothing was going to happen to it. One day when I was driving north on Highway 100, I hit an icy spot and flew across the median, across the oncoming traffic lane, and ended up in the ditch.

The car was fine, but I was so shook up David had to drive out of the ditch and back onto the highway. He insisted I drive again the next day, saying, "You have to get right back on the horse or you'll never dare to ride again." So I did drive again the next day, and eventually got my driver's license.

I certainly did not want to be like my mother who had never learned to drive a car.

David and I set our wedding date for October 4, 1958. I would not return to school for my senior year. Since my family had moved again after the end of my junior year at North High, I would have transferred to South High for my senior year anyway. Now I wouldn't have to be the new girl at school one more time.

While part of me mourned the fact that I would never go to college, the rest of me was so in love with David, and so excited about getting married, that I didn't spend much time thinking about my loss. After all, David said I didn't need an education.

I'd be a wife and mother. My mother had said my job was to be a wife and mother. How could they both be wrong?

⚊

David's sister, Lyla, living in the city, invited us to her home so I could meet some of Dave's other siblings. She served strawberry shortcake, a dessert I had never had, and I was impressed.

Some of my cousins gave me a surprise bridal shower. David was in on the surprise and had taken me out to dinner. I ordered a steak and it was too much for me to eat, so I wrapped it in a napkin and put it in my purse. We got home and, "surprise," the living room was full of women.

One of the games they played required each guest to open her purse to reveal some particular thing. I don't remember what, exactly. I protested. How could I open my purse and reveal part of a steak wrapped in a napkin? I was mortified when I was finally forced to open my purse. "You should have asked for a doggy bag," someone said. I had never heard of such a thing. I'm sure my mother hadn't either. *Would I never learn what other people already know about life?*

Mom didn't know any more about planning a wedding than I did. Mom's social circle included a few sisters and sisters-in-law who came over to drink coffee and smoke cigarettes with her at the kitchen table. "We can't afford a church wedding," she said. "Just go to the justice of the peace like we did."

I wanted a church wedding, however, but we hadn't been attending any church. I thought, why not get married at the First Augustana Lutheran Church just a couple blocks from where I lived? David agreed.

I called the church, and pastor Bernard Spong agreed to marry us on that Saturday, October 4, at eleven o'clock in the morning. David and I went to the courthouse and bought our marriage license. I asked David's sister Jane to be my maid of honor, and my sister Donna to be a bridesmaid. David's brother Rollie would be best man, and my brother Lee the groomsman.

When I looked at the price of wedding dresses at Rush's Bridal Shop on Nicollet Avenue in downtown Minneapolis, I despaired of finding one I could afford. I was working, but not earning much money. Then the clerk showed me the used dress section.

There, hanging on a hanger, was a beautiful creamy-white satin wedding dress that fit both my body and my budget. The bodice was covered with sequins and pearls. It resembled the dress my bride doll wore, except this had a long train. I put money down to hold the dress and promised to come back the following week when I got paid. I would ask David to drive me, as I couldn't carry this dress home on the bus.

When I got the dress home later that week and showed it to Mom, she had tears in her eyes. "Try it on," she said. When I did, she whispered, "You're going to be a beautiful bride."

I had also bought an inexpensive tiara at the bridal shop and a few yards of bridal veil fabric at Amluxon's fabric store. I made a bridal veil and attached the fabric to the tiara. My three sisters stared at me in wonder as I tried on the veil and looked in the mirror. "You look like Cinderella," Judie said.

David had bought the matching wedding band when he bought my engagement ring. Now I went to the same small jewelry shop and bought a plain gold band for David, requesting that our wedding date be inscribed inside. David had given me a beautiful gold cross on a delicate gold chain with our initials and wedding date inscribed on the back of the cross.

So we had the church booked for the ceremony and the reception. I had my wedding dress and veil; we had the rings and a list of guests. I had ordered the invitations, the flowers, and a wedding cake, and had hired a photographer. Now we needed to plan food for the reception. "We can't afford to pay for food for that many people," Mom said.

All my money had gone for buying my wedding dress and the invitations. Dave's money had gone for my wedding and engagement rings. What we would both earn prior to the wedding would only pay for what we had already ordered for the wedding. What would we do for food?

Dave and I went to Paynesville to visit his family that weekend, and when Dave's mother asked about our wedding plans, I told her about our reception dilemma. "Have it potluck," Dave's dad said. "That's what people do around here."

I couldn't believe it. People bringing food to a wedding reception? But I had only been to one wedding. At my cousin Ruthie's wedding, we didn't bring food. Her mother had their dining room table loaded with beautiful dishes of food and people filled their plates and ate outside in their back yard. "Is it okay to ask people to bring food to a wedding?" I asked.

"Sure," Russell said. "I don't think it would be any different in the city. Everybody does potluck around here all the time."

When I got home, I told Mom what Russell had said about potluck. "That sounds like a good idea," Mom said. "Just add a note in with the wedding invitations asking people to bring a dish to pass.

So that's what I did.

CHAPTER THIRTY-ONE
POTLUCK WEDDING

Our wedding day, October 4, 1958, arrived crisp and sunny. Since the wedding wasn't until eleven o'clock, I went for a walk in the morning to settle my nerves. I knew I was doing the right thing. I just wanted it all to go well.

When my dad walked me down the aisle of First Augustana Lutheran Church in his new gray suit and tie, the church was full of people. Jane and Donna wore long dresses of soft blue organza and carried bouquets of cascading carnations. The men wore black tuxedos, black bow ties, and boutonnières of white carnations. Our mothers wore corsages of pink baby roses. David's mom wore a dark blue dress and hat. Mom was lovely in a light beige dress and hat, though she didn't believe me when I told her so.

My wedding dress fit me perfectly, and I carried a cascade of pink roses and carnations. The cross David had given me hung around my neck, and my "something borrowed" was the pearl earrings I wore. "Something blue" was my garter. I trembled with realization of the magnitude of what I was doing as I held Dad's arm and walked down the aisle, trying to somehow keep time with the music. But the expression on David's smiling face, and the peace in my heart, confirmed that I was doing the right thing.

David and I stood together at the altar, my hand in David's, and pastor Spong said, "We stand before God ..." I nearly gulped.

Yes, we stood before my Heavenly Father at that moment. Yet I had not thanked Him for giving me this wonderful man as my husband. I had not asked Him if David was the right man for me. I had not asked a blessing upon our marriage. I had been so caught up in falling in love, being in love, and planning this wedding that I had forgotten about Him entirely.

Pastor Spong was still talking and I forced myself to listen. We said our vows and exchanged wedding rings. David kissed me when given permission to do so. After the receiving line, we posed with our parents and the wedding party for professional photos. Then we joined our guests at the reception.

I had ordered a beautiful wedding cake. I don't remember what other food we ate, but we had food, so at least some of our guests brought a dish to pass. No one told me that was not the proper thing to do. I didn't hear that anyone refused our invitation because they were asked to bring a dish to pass. Neither did anyone give us an etiquette book as a wedding gift.

I have attended many weddings since that day, both in the city and in the country. None were potluck. Even now, so many years later, I cringe every time I recall the potluck part of our wedding.

At the wedding reception, after we ate and opened our many gifts, I tossed my garter. The guests sprayed us with rice as we left the church. Someone had written *Just Married* on David's car and had tied cans on the back, so we made a lot of noise as we took off.

David and I changed clothes at Mom and Dad's house, picked up our suitcases, and drove toward the North Shore of Lake Superior where we would spend several days honeymooning. I felt almost happy, yet nervous. We were married! *Will I be a good wife?*

I was excited about seeing Lake Superior for the first time. While various thoughts ran through my mind, underneath it all, my thoughts turned to my Heavenly Father—how faithful He had been.

How long had it been since I had talked to my Heavenly Father? I had been so busy going to school, dating, working, and planning a wedding lately that I had taken Him for granted. I consistently felt His presence. I always knew He loved me. I knew He was there when I needed Him. But, although I held Him close, I had neglected to talk to Him, to tell Him that I loved Him, or to ask for His guidance with all my plans for quite a while.

He was still my secret. Lee was the only one who knew I had accepted Christ that night, but he never mentioned it and neither did I. Except for the few confirmation classes I attended, I had never learned anything more about my Heavenly Father. None of my family or friends ever mentioned Him. I didn't have a Bible. But, though I had never shared Him with anyone, He remained very real to me.

I realized that David was a gift from my secret Father in Heaven. I could never have found a man as good as David on my own. *Thank you, Heavenly Father.* My heart filled with enormous love for my Heavenly Father. He loved me, and I trusted Him with my life. David also loved me and I trusted David with my life. It was time to share my secret Father in Heaven with David. I looked at David driving the car beside me. He turned and smiled at me. "David," I said. "I have a secret that I want to tell you. A secret I have had since I was nine years old."

CHAPTER THIRTY-TWO

THE FARM

After we were married we rented a furnished third-floor apartment on Eighteenth Street and Chicago Avenue in South Minneapolis. About five months later I realized I was pregnant. We moved to a less expensive one-room, third-floor, furnished studio apartment at 1825 Park Avenue South because we decided to buy the 170-acre farm for sale near where David grew up. We wanted to quickly save money for the down payment.

On November 5, 1959, at 7:52 p.m., one year, one month, and one day after our wedding, our first daughter, Laura Lee, was born at St. Barnabas Hospital. Laura weighed eight pounds, four ounces and was twenty-one inches long. She was beautiful, with a head full of dark hair. I was eighteen and David was twenty-five.

After I came home from the hospital, to save even more money for the farm, we moved in with my parents. But a few months later, we found a place on Franklin Avenue for reasonable rent, and moved there.

Dave was working night shift at the hospital then. One evening when he was working, I got a babysitter for Laura and went with Donna to see the Alfred Hitchcock movie, *Psycho*. The movie frightened me so badly that I made Donna stay with me that night. Even my Heavenly Father was not enough comfort after that movie.

David changed to day shift, and I went back to work at the hospital as a nurse's aide again. David cared for Laura while I worked nights. We felt like we saw each other only in passing, but we soon had enough money for a down payment on the farm near Paynesville. We bought 170 acres for $25,000. We moved to the farm in 1960. By that time I was pregnant with our second daughter.

Elderly bachelors had built the house on the farm after their original farmhouse had burned, but they never finished the inside. It was so dirty that we moved into the second story of the house while we cleaned and finished the first floor. The upstairs had a bedroom with a slanted ceiling, but it was large enough for a double bed and crib. We used the slanted ceiling area on the other side of the upstairs as a makeshift kitchen with a hot plate, orange crates for cupboards, and a small refrigerator. With no plumbing coming upstairs, we carried our water up from the main floor. Memories of our tarpaper shack in Montana came to mind.

The center part of the upstairs was our living room. We had an old couch someone had given us. I wasn't used to luxury, and we were too much in love to complain about anything. We lived on faith and hope for a better future while we slowly cleaned, painted, and furnished the main floor so we could occupy the whole house.

We began attending Nordland Lutheran Church in rural Paynesville, and I finally began to find answers to my questions about my Heavenly Father. I learned that He is God. Over the years, I had often wondered whether Jesus was my Heavenly Father. I learned that Jesus is God's son. Did that make Jesus my brother? Wow! That was mind-boggling! It wasn't difficult to understand the Holy Trinity because I had learned about Jesus in Sunday school long ago. I could easily accept the Holy Spirit as the presence I always clearly felt.

Some of what I learned was easy to understand, and some of it was confusing. Was it God who was with me all the time, or was it the Holy Spirit? I decided to keep praying to my Heavenly Father the same as I always had. I knew He heard me and He answered me. He helped me. He comforted me. He knew me.

I cried when I learned that my Heavenly Father had sent his own son, Jesus, to die for our sins. I cried for my Father's pain and for the terrible pain that Jesus endured. We don't deserve that sacrifice. David had a Bible that he received when he was confirmed, and I began to read it. Much of what I read was difficult to understand, but I learned more with each sermon I heard. Once again, I loved attending church.

We had Laura baptized. Since neither David nor I had been baptized, we were baptized at the same time. David and I began saying grace before each meal. We brought my Heavenly Father into the open and into our home. That pleased me so much.

I painted the bathroom yellow—such a bright yellow that one's eyes flew open the minute one stepped inside. I learned that a little yellow goes a long way.

The kitchen had no built-in cabinets, so we bought an old, used, pie safe for a cupboard. I stripped the many layers of wallpaper from the interior before painting the whole thing white. We bought a used gas stove, a refrigerator, and a table with four chairs. After I made red-and-white checkered curtains and a matching tablecloth, I thought the kitchen was beautiful.

We bought an oak rocker for fifty cents in Minneapolis and refinished it. We moved the old couch from upstairs into our living room, and also bought a used floor lamp. By today's standards, it wasn't much, but we felt blessed in our cozy home and on our own farm.

David built fencing and bought young cattle and farm machinery on credit to begin farming. But he also found a fulltime job to see us through until the farm began paying. It made for long days and hard weekends, but David loved it. He finally had his own farm—a lifetime dream come true.

Dave worked for Irvin Beal as a laborer doing jackhammer and cement work. He also painted a high church steeple when they couldn't get anyone else to climb that high. When work became scarce with Beal, he was hired by St. Regis Paper Company in Sartell and worked there all winter.

Elaine Donna was born on March 24, 1961, at 3:27 a.m. at Paynesville Community Hospital. Dr. Thomas Vanderpool delivered her. She too was beautiful with a head full of dark hair. Laura was only sixteen months old, still in diapers, and only barely walking.

When spring came, Dave and all the other employees were laid off from the paper company due to no work. We were deep in debt, and even had a huge bill at the general store for groceries.

David had bought me a wringer washing machine at an auction sale. With no water heater, I filled the washer with a hose from the sink and heated the water by means of an electric donut placed in the water. I filled galvanized tubs with cold water for rinsing.

When the agitator broke, David wired it together. Sometimes clothes got caught and tore. Our water was also full of iron, and our clothes became streaked with orange after being washed. Hence, after washday, our clothes often looked worse than before. I had two babies and this was the pre-disposable-diaper era.

One day, the wringer broke completely. Already several diapers and one blouse had been torn, the clothes were orange from the iron in the water, and I had had it. I was so angry that I shoved that washing machine, water and all, out the door and down the steps. I watched it clunk down one step after another and land at the bottom of the stairs, water sloshing left and right as it went.

When Dave came home that night he wondered if he should throw his hat in first to see if it too would come flying out. We have laughed about that incident many times over the years, but it wasn't one bit funny that day.

I was pregnant again. I had been using an IUD for birth control, but obviously it wasn't foolproof. When Dr. Vanderpool told me I was pregnant again I began to cry. *How could we afford another baby?* He said, "You should be happy you are having another baby. You have such beautiful babies." It didn't make me feel better.

While David was laid off, we were so broke that I decided to help earn some money. Elaine was only a few months old, but I took a job selling Playhouse Toys by party plan. Dave cared for Laura and Elaine during the evenings when I held toy parties at other people's homes.

I earned money that fall and got free toys for the girls, but I was pregnant again and was sleep deprived. One night as I drove home from a toy party, I briefly fell asleep at the wheel. I awoke as I hit something in my path. It was a large empty cardboard box, so neither the car nor I were injured. My Heavenly Father was certainly watching over me again. It scared me so badly, however, that I decided with two babies at home and being pregnant again, it was too much for me to be working nights.

It was lonely living at the farm. I missed my family. We couldn't afford a telephone and I didn't have a car when Dave was at work. I realized how Mom must have felt with Dad gone so much of the time when she was stuck at home with the children without a phone or car. I leaned heavily on my Heavenly Father, but Mom hadn't had that comfort.

Mom and Dad and my sisters came to visit us once in a while. On one visit, Irene showed me a picture of Dad ice-skating with her and Lee. Jealousy gripped my chest so hard I could hardly breathe. Dad had never done anything with me. Ever. Another picture showed Dad and Lee playing checkers. I should have been happy for Lee and Irene that they were getting some time and attention from Dad, but it was hard to be happy for them when my eyes were clouded and my breathing difficult.

Was Dad finally noticing that he had children? Did Dad care more for them than he had for me? Maybe he had more time on his hands now that they lived in a home that required less maintenance and he owned a vehicle that required fewer repairs. Perhaps now that I am married and gone from home, he realizes that we grow up quickly and he wants to spend some time with the others before they too are gone. Whatever the reason, it was a shock to see those pictures and see Dad as a different person than the one I grew up with.

David got a job at a machine shop and began working days again. Soon afterward, on May 25, 1962, Lisa Marie was born at Paynesville. She weighed nine pounds, eleven and a half ounces and was twenty-three inches long. Dr. Vanderpool said, "Didn't I tell you that you had beautiful babies?" And she was beautiful. She looked so much like Laura. I loved her immediately. But I was only twenty years old and I had three children under the age of three. Elaine wasn't even walking yet.

Maybe that is why I suffered post-partum depression after Lisa was born. I was sad all the time. But I didn't know that it was a physical ailment and there may have been help for me. Therefore, I suffered for many weeks, praying to my Heavenly Father to make me feel happy again. One morning I awoke and everything felt different—I felt energetic and the sun was shining beautifully. I hadn't noticed the sun for a long time, although I'm sure it had shone. I felt happy. I was me again. I thanked my Heavenly Father for making me happy again.

One day David's boss drove into our farmyard to tell me that David was in the hospital. A band saw had cut off two of his fingers at the machine shop. Someone was astute enough to wrap his severed fingers in a cloth and bring them to the hospital. The doctors sewed his fingers back on, but he was unable to return to work. We had been holding on by our fingertips as it was. Now what?

While we prayed for Dave's recovery, our farm, and the ability to pay our bills, we were forced to admit that we were not making it on the farm. We trusted God to provide, but we knew we had to do our part. We were so deep in debt that we couldn't dig ourselves out.

That was the beginning of the end of our farming. We would have to return to the city. David was devastated.

Me—not so much.

CHAPTER THIRTY-THREE

BACK TO THE CITY

David sold the cattle and machinery to pay off most of our bills. We listed the farm for sale, and Dave went to Minneapolis to look for work. He stayed with his sister, Lyla, and her family that week. It had been a lonely and difficult week for me, alone with our three little girls. But I didn't realize that the week had been equally difficult for David until he arrived home on Friday and we cried in each other's arms. "I'm not going back Sunday without you and the girls," he said. "I missed you too much."

With David determined that we stay together while he looked for work, and with no place to go when we arrived in Minneapolis that Sunday, we decided to try the furnished apartments we had lived in when we were first married four years earlier. Within minutes we were unloading our old '36 Chevy pickup of cribs, high chair, and clothing. We had taken only what we needed until we could get established in a house.

I tried to acclimate myself to what I knew were only temporary quarters, but it was difficult living in that drab, dreary apartment. When we lived there before I had made pretty curtains and sofa pillows and placed family photos on the wall. Now I had none of our personal belongings to make it cozy.

Also, the whole building had gone downhill since we lived there before. An older couple that lived in the apartment next door was usually so drunk they could barely climb the stairs. One day the wife was lying on the landing. I helped her climb the last flight of stairs to the third floor. When she opened the door to their apartment I saw only a bare room. It looked even worse than ours.

David found temporary work at a Clark service station working nights so he could look for a permanent job during the day. He also worked weekends at a car wash and all night Saturday at the *Minneapolis Star and Tribune* office assembling the Sunday newspaper. I stayed busy caring for our three babies at home.

Even though David worked three jobs, we still couldn't afford luxuries like a telephone because getting our bills paid was our priority. I felt isolated in those ugly surroundings where the dirty windows faced the brick wall of the next building only a few feet away. Often, when all three of my babies cried at the same time, I cried too.

The bills we hadn't been able to pay kept coming in the mail. I hated seeing PAST DUE in red ink. I remembered Mom's voice; "We didn't have money, so we left our things there for the landlord to sell to pay for the rent." *Would we have to leave our things at home to help pay for the farm?*

One night I asked David, "When are we going to sell the farm? I can't stand this place. There's no beauty here. I need something pretty to look at. It's almost Christmas and we don't even have Christmas decorations to put up."

David held me in his arms and assured me that he would find a permanent job soon and then we could look for a house to rent. "Then I'll go back to the farm and get the rest of our things," he said. "Soon, honey, soon," he assured me.

A few days later I answered a knock at the door with Lisa in my arms. There stood the alcoholic couple from next door. I never did know their names. They were sober for a change, dressed in many layers of clothing, eyes baggy, cheeks hollow. They each hung on to a large, green duffel bag.

"We're movin' out," he said. "We wanted to say ga'-bye."

"We want you to have this," she quickly added, handing me a Santa elf made from Styrofoam balls, red felt, and colorful sequins.

"Thank you," I said, accepting the gift from her shaky hand. "It's beautiful. I've been needing something pretty to look at."

Her bloodshot eyes took in the baby in my arms and my other two daughters standing close to me, shyly hugging my legs. Then she looked back at me. "You have three pretty little faces to look at every day," she said, speaking each word distinctly for effect.

"Yes," he agreed. "Nuthin's more bootiful than those little gals a'yours. God bless ya, now." He nodded to me as she smiled sadly. Then they turned around to the stairs and held the rail tightly as she followed him, their only belongings making a thud with each step they descended.

On that cold day in December of 1962, I stood in the open doorway and watched them leaving their home. I looked again at the bright red Santa elf in my hand. *Why did they give me this gift? They barely know me.*

It was several minutes before the full realization of our neighbors' situation hit me. They had no place to go. They were probably evicted because they couldn't pay the rent. I wanted to call them back. I wanted to say, "We have room for you." But they were gone.

Memories of a long-ago gift of hand-embroidered pillowcases came to mind. My Heavenly Father had used those neighbors to give us hope. *Did He use these neighbors to give me hope again?* I had been feeling sorry for myself, but they showed me how blessed I am. We still live in a warm, safe apartment. I have three beautiful, healthy children. I have a wonderful, hardworking husband who loves me. We would be okay.

I sat on the sofa and gathered my children around me. "See what our Daddy in Heaven gave us?" I asked the wide-eyed little girls who looked at the colorful elf in my hand. "Daddy is going to get a good job, and we are going to sell the farm and pay all our bills, and then some day we will have another house—a nice house.

As I hugged the girls close to me, I knew what I said was true. My Heavenly Father had told me so. I had begun to recognize when and how He spoke to me.

CHAPTER THIRTY-FOUR

OUR FAMILY IS COMPLETE

In March 1963, David got a job at Northern States Power Company working nights in the garage. We moved to a rented house at 2211 Tenth Avenue South in Minneapolis. I took a job as waitress at Keller Drugstore on Fourteenth and Chicago Avenue working days so that David could care for the girls. Again, we felt like we saw each other in passing. But we had many bills to pay off from our time at the farm. Later I was promoted to clerk.

On November 22, I was standing on a chair hanging draperies I had made for the front windows. David had gone to redeem some Gold Bond Stamps. When he came home, his face showed something was terribly wrong. "President Kennedy's been shot," he said. I got down from the chair and turned on the television. We watched it in shock for most of the rest of the day. I prayed for Jackie and her children as my heart went out to her.

One day Laura was playing outside and she stepped on a piece of glass on the sidewalk. The glass was too deeply imbedded in her foot for me to remove it. I had no car to take her to the doctor, so a neighbor woman who saw what was happening offered to drive us to the emergency room of the hospital. I wasn't well acquainted with this woman, but had seen her a few times. She was telling another neighbor that she was going to take us to the hospital, and I heard her say, "It's one of those *clean* little girls." It made me realize that most of the other kids in that neighborhood were usually rather dirty looking, but yes, I did keep our girls clean.

I also realized how nice it was to be acquainted with neighbors. I was grateful for the help I had received without a moment's hesitation. I felt willing to help anyone else if I could. I thought about how reticent Mom was about getting acquainted with neighbors, and I wondered why she felt that way. I decided that she missed a lot of happiness because of that attitude, and I wasn't going to follow in her footsteps in that regard.

In 1964, David was transferred to the overhead department of NSP as grounds man. He began training at Dunwoody Institute to learn to be a journeyman lineman. With that good job we began looking for a house to rent in the country. We wanted to get out of the city. We found a rent-free caretaker situation on a farm near Hanover owned by George and Doris Hedlund. We were thrilled to live in that old farm house with a long driveway and lots of yard and woodlands.

We joined St. Paul's Lutheran Church in Hanover, and once again I was learning more and more about my Heavenly Father. I hadn't been reading the Bible much, but I was listening carefully to the sermons and Bible readings on Sundays. David joined the choir. With three little children to care for, I always had a child on my lap and had little time for myself. We became acquainted with many of the families in the community. Eventually I was helping to teach summer Bible school.

The following year Laura began first grade. She looked so proud to be going to school in her red and green plaid dress and brown jacket and cap I had sewn for her. We didn't have bus service until the following year, so I drove Laura to school. I only shed a few tears at my first baby being grown up enough to go to school.

The old farmhouse we lived in left a lot to be desired. Although David was working a steady job, his income didn't stretch far enough for any extras. We were still trying to pay off our farm bills. I wanted a record player so we could enjoy music. I also wanted to redecorate our living room. So David and I discussed my working and I got a job in St. Louis Park doing waitress work at the Boulevard Restaurant. Again, David got home from work and I left to go to work about three evenings a week.

David was a wonderful husband. He was young, strong, and energetic. He grew up in the tradition that the women care for the household and the children and the men earn a living and care for the outside and the equipment. Although he didn't like it, he did his best to accommodate my working outside the house and earning some of the money.

I made good tips at The Boulevard and I soon bought a record player and a few records. One of the first records we bought was "Red Rubber Ball" by The Seekers. The girls and I held hands and danced around the living room when I played that song. We enjoyed the music that record player provided for us for many, many years.

The food trays at The Boulevard were heavy and serving food was hard work, so I became a cocktail waitress instead. I got a job at Michael's Supper Club in Golden Valley. Again, the tips were good. When I saved enough money, I called Dayton's Department Store and asked to have an interior designer come out. I made cinnamon rolls and timed them so they would be almost done baking at the time the designer, John Thill, arrived. When he got there, I told him, "I want our house to look just like it smells right now." He got the message.

He was wonderful to work with. He guided me, but allowed me to use my own taste in choosing colors and fabrics. We worked around what we already had—a blue sofa, an oak rocker, an old upright piano, and an antique pie safe. We selected small-print wallpaper in a rich, cream color and I wallpapered the living room. I painted the wainscoting a nice blue to go with our sofa. I ordered custom-made gold-colored draperies and valances with gold trim. They tied back to reveal beautiful white sheers.

I ordered enough extra drapery fabric and trim to make a floor-length tablecloth for the large round end table David made from an empty wire spool he got from work. I "antiqued" the pie safe a distressed blue with gold interior and put chicken wire inside the glass windows. Other expenditures were two table lamps and gold carpeting. When we were done, the living room did have the cozy feeling of warm, homemade, cinnamon rolls. I absolutely loved that room the rest of the time we lived there.

David still talked about wanting a son. I was on birth control pills. After the living room was done, I decided I was ready to have another baby, hopefully a son this time. I stopped taking the pills and in no time at all I was pregnant. Cynthia Anne was born May 13, 1966, at 1:45 p.m. at the Buffalo Hospital. She weighed seven pounds, eleven ounces and was eighteen inches long.

Cindy was a beautiful baby with a full head of dark hair like each of the other girls. Although we had both hoped for a boy, we were delighted with yet another girl. I was in the hospital for about five days. When Dave came to take me home, he had all three of the other girls with him. They were happy to see the baby and me, and were full of questions and comments all the way home. They kept reaching over the seat to touch us and get a better look at the baby. It was wonderful to see them again, but by the time we arrived home I was exhausted. I walked into the kitchen and saw that the floor was dirty. I said, "The floor is dirty," and I began crying.

Poor David! He didn't understand why I cried just because the kitchen floor was dirty. I was only twenty-four and I had a husband, a house, and four little children to care for. He didn't realize I was so weak and tired that the thought of meeting the needs of all of them was overwhelming at that moment.

After a few days recovery, I felt the warmth and satisfaction of motherhood once again. I recognized that having a husband, a house, and four little children was a *huge* blessing from my Heavenly Father, and I trusted He would give me the strength and wisdom to care for them as they deserved and He intended. My children were all normal and healthy, and as others had pointed out, they were all beautiful. Our family was complete.

I had safely reached adulthood. I was doing what my mother expected of me—I had become a wife and a mother. Now all I had to do was raise my children to be healthy, happy, productive women. I had so much responsibility, and I knew so little about how to be a good parent and a good wife.

I prayed often to my Heavenly Father for guidance.

CHAPTER THIRTY-FIVE

COLLEGE

We loved living on the Hedland farm. George and Doris, and their daughter Holly, built a house for themselves on the other side of the barn and used it as sort of a weekend and party place. They kept to themselves when they were there, and we did the same. But they were good to us. The summer when Cindy was a baby and the weather was extremely hot and humid, they bought us an air conditioner. When the children got a little older, they put in a cement patio for us and bought us some redwood patio furniture.

The girls grew fast and played well together. I continued to work part-time evenings, but I was becoming restless doing waitress work. I didn't like being away from home in the evenings. I decided to do sewing and alterations for others.

Soon I had a good client base with many satisfied customers. I made wedding and bridesmaid dresses, little girls' dance costumes, and business suits for a woman with severe scoliosis who could not buy ready-made suits. I altered beautiful wool Pendleton shirts for a man with short arms, and shortened pants for both men and women. I put in new zippers, patched pants, shortened skirts, and basically sewed whatever my clients needed. My problem was I didn't charge enough. I wasn't making much money.

I registered with a temporary job agency and was only sent on menial jobs that required no skill. And I made very little money. I decided I needed an education after all.

So at the age of twenty-nine, I took my high school equivalency tests (GED exams). If prep classes were offered back then, I didn't know about it. I went in cold, after being out of school for twelve years, and took the exams in two days. The first day I tested on history and math, my worst subjects in school. I left the college, walked out into a beautiful, warm, fall day and my teeth began chattering together uncontrollably. I couldn't make them stop.

I decided that if I got something to eat and drink, maybe I could relax and the chattering would stop, so I pulled into a drive-in restaurant. It was so embarrassing when I tried to order a soft drink and a hot dog. The carhop looked at me as if I was a lunatic. But after eating and drinking with some difficulty, I finally relaxed enough that I became normal again. Then I only had to worry that I might not have passed the tests.

The next day I was tested in literature, English, and social studies. I felt confident in those areas. The woman who gave me my test results said she had never graded an English paper with a higher score than mine. Those three high-score tests compensated for the lower scores on the other tests. I passed! Now I could go to college.

In September 1970 I became a full-time student at North Hennepin Community College. Surprisingly, I wasn't the only adult student there. I loved it! On some days I even took Cindy to classes with me. On other days I took her to Joan Polston, a dear friend, who cared for her while I was in school. I arranged for my classes to be held in the mornings so I could be home in the afternoons and evenings with my family. I did homework at the kitchen table with my three school-age daughters.

It wasn't easy being a full-time college student, a wife, and a mother with a house and gardens to care for, but I managed. David wasn't thrilled that I was going to college, but he didn't object unless I mentioned being tired or overworked, so I learned to keep that to myself.

I graduated in December 1972 with an Associate in Science Degree, and began working as a paralegal for Ed Winer, attorney-at-law, in January 1973. I would be earning $1,000 a month to start.

CHAPTER THIRTY-SIX

WORKING GIRL

I was nervous about that first day of work. I would be working on the twenty-third floor of the new IDS Building in downtown Minneapolis for the prestigious law firm of Van Valkenburg, Comaford, Moss, Fassett, Flaherty, and Clarkson.

We wore Kickareenos back then, warm furry boots that are worn without shoes. We carried our shoes in a zippered bag so we could change when we came indoors. I was so afraid I would forget my shoes and have to spend the whole day in those hot boots. Well, I am happy to report I did not forget my shoes. I forgot my purse!

There I was, new at the office, with no lipstick and no money to pay for my parking at the end of the day. Thank goodness I brought my lunch. I had to borrow money from one of the secretaries. I never forgot my purse again.

I loved that job. I met the attorney's secretarial needs as well as drafted legal documents and met with clients for some of their needs. Clients were charged $35 per hour for my time.

In 1974, George Hedlund sold the farm we lived on to Bob Dylan, the singer. Bob requested we stay on as caretakers, but we had already anticipated having to move and had found a home we fell in love with, so we declined his offer.

Our new five-bedroom home was on a small lake between Hanover and St. Michael. It cost $40,000. Each of our four girls had their own bedroom and we had two bathrooms. What a luxury!

Later that year it became too difficult to be working so far from the girls. It took an hour to drive each way, and I had started carpooling to save money, so it then became impossible to get home during the day if the girls needed me. That didn't happen often, but after an especially difficult day of Cindy being sick and crying for me, I decided to find a job closer to home. I left the law firm and took a job working for Wyman Nelson, the county attorney in Buffalo.

A year later, being frustrated with not having much responsibility or the freedom to work on my own, I left the county attorney's office and went back to the city to work for a patent law attorney at International Multifoods in downtown Minneapolis.

While I had been working at the county attorney's office I had applied for a job as a county court reporter at Wright County, but had heard nothing. In October of that year, they called me for an interview and I was hired. I became the county court reporter for three judges. I made good money, worked independently, and had lots of responsibility—all the things I wanted in a job.

My many job changes made me wonder about my father. He changed jobs frequently. What was he looking for in a job? Did he ever find it? He seemed happiest when he and Mom lived in the country between Onamia and Milaca and Dad raised pigs. But Mom was unhappy there. My sister Donna and her husband bought a house in Hopkins, and Mom and Dad moved into that house. Dad drove a delivery truck for Bachman's Nursery and he did a lot of gardening. He loved gardening, especially the flowers. I guess he just liked being close to nature, and I think if he could have done so, he would have farmed his whole life.

As Dad got older, he became much more sentimental and he cried easily. I guess that's where I get that from. He cried at church, at baptisms and confirmation of our daughters, at Christmas, at Easter, and at birthday celebrations. Did he ever accept Christ into his life? I don't know.

Why didn't I ever share my faith with him?

CHAPTER THIRTY-SEVEN

GOD IS WATCHING OVER ME

I was running late that fall morning in 1975 as I slid behind the wheel of our turquoise 1970 Cutlass Oldsmobile. She was smooth and shiny inside as well as outside. You know how cars were back then—before bucket seats, center armrests, seat belts, or airbags. Just a long stretch of smooth slippery vinyl upholstery—across the whole seat.

It was a twelve-mile drive to my job as county court reporter. David was an electrical lineman. David and I were both busy outside our fulltime jobs. Living as caretakers on a hobby farm, David cared for the dogs, horses, and the grounds, while I cared for our home, our children, and the gardens. I sewed our children's clothes and canned garden vegetables while David cut wood for the fireplace, hoed the garden, plowed the snow, and kept the vehicles in good repair. David sang in the church choir and I taught Bible school at St. Paul's Lutheran Church in Hanover.

We were much blessed, but we were feeling the stress of trying to do too much. It seemed as if we were rushing all the time. Even now, as I glanced out the window of the car, I could see that the countryside was glorious! Swaying leaves of yellow, orange, and red danced with the morning sun. Soft dew still glistened on the ground in places, winking at me shyly as I glanced their way. Yet I sped around the curves too fast to take much notice, trying to get to work on time.

After several miles, I remembered my daily chat with God. But, feeling rushed, I kept it brief. *"Thank you, Lord, for this day! Thank you for my wonderful husband and our four healthy daughters. Be with each of us this day and keep us safe. In Jesus name, Amen."*

I rounded a curve and saw two little boys walking from their house toward the highway, little metal lunch boxes in their hands. I reached for the brake, knowing I was driving too fast. At the same time their black Lab dashed onto the highway in front of me. I did what we are always told to not do—I veered to avoid hitting the dog. The Lab tried to stop, but skidded under my car. I heard a sickening thud as the dog rolled over and over beneath me. *The children are watching their dog being killed.* I felt heartsick!

I was almost in the ditch on my right side so I turned left holding onto the steering wheel as best I could while sliding around on the slippery seat. I headed toward the opposite ditch—a deep ditch! Out of the corner of my eye I saw the dog running back to the house. *Thank you, God.*

I bounced up as the car lurched down into the ditch and hit ground, then continued fast over uneven ground. I was headed straight for a pasture of goats. As I sped toward the goats, they turned and looked at me with the most ridiculous look of shock on their faces. Then they scattered like bowling pins. It looked so funny I laughed. Here I was, my car completely out of control while I headed into a wooded area—and I was laughing! Even at the time, I realized how strange that was.

"Put your foot on the brake," said a voice from the back seat.

"What?" I answered as I tried to maintain control of the car while it dipped and bounced forward.

"Put your foot on the brake," the voice repeated from behind my right shoulder.

I looked down and realized for the first time, while I had a tight grip on the steering wheel, my body had slid over to the passenger side. Both feet were on the passenger side of the center hump on the floor, far from the brake pedal. I quickly pulled my body back to the driver's position, found the brakes, and stopped the car. I was two feet short of crashing into a large oak tree!

I sat there stunned for a few minutes before I found the strength to reach up and put the car in park. Then I slowly turned my head and looked behind me. I knew no one was in the back seat, but *someone* had spoken to me, twice, clearly and calmly, from the back seat.

Just five minutes before the dog ran into my path, I had prayed, "Keep us safe, Lord." When the mother of the two little boys came running to the car, her pink robe flying open as she called, "Are you all right? Are you all right?" all I could think of was God's promise in Psalm 91:11 … *For he will command his angels concerning you to guard you in all your ways.* (NIV)

God had placed an angel in the back seat to keep me safe that day. I believe He was also telling me to slow down—not just on the highway, but in my life. I drove the rest of the way to work at a leisurely pace, talking to my Heavenly Father as I drove. Then, instead of immediately starting dinner when I got home that night, I asked my daughters to sit down and tell me about their day. Then I told them about the angel who saved my life.

CHAPTER THIRTY-EIGHT

BAD TIMES

I liked my job as court reporter, but that industry was changing. A new law required all court reporters, both county court and district court, to be machine reporters. I did all my court reporting by shorthand with a tape backup. I would either have to give up my job or learn machine reporting. So I went back to school to learn machine reporting. Dave didn't agree with that decision, but then, we hadn't been agreeing on much lately.

Twice a week, I drove into Minneapolis after work and attended school. I also spent at least two hours each evening and more on the weekends practicing on the machine. With four noisy children in the house, in order to concentrate, I went into the upstairs bathroom and instructed the girls to not bother me unless they were bleeding.

One day I was holed up in the bathroom, trying to bring my speed up to the necessary requirement, when I heard a sheet of paper being slipped under the door. I picked it up and read, "Mom, can I please go to Tony's house to play? Love, Cindy."

My heart felt as if it was being squeezed in the vice David had in the garage. I had to fight back tears. What was I doing?

My precious daughters were growing up on the other side of the bathroom door while I put my job before them. My priorities were all mixed up!

I opened the door, hugged Cindy, and quit court reporting school. David had been right this time. But between both our jobs and raising four girls, our lives were often stressful. We hardly communicated with each other unless it was about the children.

In 1978, when the new court reporting law went into effect, I left Wright County and got a job as paralegal for Michael Swirnoff at the Leonard, Street, and Deinard law firm in downtown Minneapolis.

Dad died on August 25 of that year. He had always had a fear of having a stroke like his father and several of his uncles. "I pray to God I'll die quickly, and not lay for months unable to care for myself," he said more than once. So I was comforted when he died suddenly of an aortic aneurysm. He was sixty-five years old. He was rarely sick and only went to the doctor when he had a gallbladder attack. He went to a dentist once when he needed a tooth pulled. Otherwise, Dad was a healthy man. I was shocked by his sudden death.

Ironically, when I was sixty-three, I needed to have an aortic valve replaced, and I too had an aortic aneurysm that needed repair. Had I not had other medical issues, it would not have been discovered. I would have died of my aortic aneurysm before now.

In 1980, I got a call from David Fricke, an acquaintance from the courthouse. He told me he was leaving his job to become the Director of the Minnesota Association of Townships. He offered me a job as his assistant. Another job change, but I would be working close to home again. I had to take a cut in pay, but I accepted. I worked independently, I had much responsibility, and I was learning many new things. I loved my job.

Things had not been good between David and me for a long time. He drank excessively and we became strangers. As a result, in March of 1981, I moved out with Cindy and rented a house in town. I knew that David would be totally devastated if he lost the house he had put so much work into, so we moved.

It wasn't an easy decision. I never thought I would be getting divorced. Shortly before the divorce became final, David asked to see me so he could ask me something. I knew he would ask me to come back to him. All day long, I struggled with my decision all over again.

That evening he came to the little yellow house where Cindy, who was still at home, and I lived and sat in the oak rocking chair where I had nursed all our children. He said, "Connie, I still love you and I miss you. I will always love you. Please come back to me."

I looked at him, so much a part of my life, sitting in that chair that was such an intimate piece of furniture, and I tried to imagine being together again. I knew he was a good man. I knew he loved me. But he was still drinking, and I couldn't deal with that. We had grown so far apart that I couldn't feel love for him anymore. I felt empty. As difficult as it was, I said, "no."

"Then, I'm going to marry Sharon," he said.

"Listen to what you're saying," I said. "That's not fair to either of you."

"I love her," David defended. "Not like I love you, but I need someone."

Our divorce was final on November 19, 1981. David and Sharon were married shortly thereafter.

Much later I learned Lisa had taken one of my aprons that had been hanging in the kitchen after she learned that I was leaving. "I needed something from our life together as a family in that house," she told me. That statement took my breath away. I felt like such a terrible mother.

I was surprised to learn how hard our divorce was on the girls. I didn't think it would be because they knew how unhappy I was. I think our divorce was hardest on Lisa. She was in college when I told them I was leaving their dad. It was about that time that Lisa quit school. Much later she told me that she felt as if her life fell apart along with her family. Laura was already married, and Lani was in college. She got married the following year. They were both more established in their lives. Lisa was in a more vulnerable place in her life. I was so mired in my own problems that I didn't recognize hers and she felt I was not available to her. Cindy was in her sophomore year of high school and still with me. Since we didn't move far, she was able to continue attending her same high school. I was almost forty years old.

Where was God during that turbulent time in my life? He was right beside me, but I was turning my back to Him. I knew He wanted me to try harder to keep my marriage intact. I didn't want to. I felt lonely and ignored by David and he refused to go to counseling or to quit drinking. I didn't want to work at it anymore. It was easier to just leave. I wanted out. So I left.

Putting my own happiness before the happiness and needs of my daughters is one of the biggest regrets I carry with me. The other is choosing divorce instead of working hard to restore my marriage to David.

CHAPTER THIRTY-NINE

STARTING OVER

"**W**hy don't you go out with some of your friends?" Cindy asked me more than once as she headed out the door for one activity or another. "I hate to see you sitting home alone all the time."

I wasn't ready to be social yet after leaving David. In fact, by the time I got home from work I was exhausted. I finally went to the doctor. "You need a hysterectomy," he said. "But, we're going to draw more blood and do this test again. I don't think it was an accurate reading." After testing me again, he said, "You tested the same. Your hemoglobin is extremely low. I can't believe you are able to go to work every day. You need to build up your blood before surgery."

Decades later, I wondered whether having such low blood, and no energy, contributed to my decision to leave David. If I had felt stronger, would I have been more willing to work to restore my marriage? I'll never know.

I am ashamed to say during that dark period of my life, when I lost touch with God, I was the president of our church council. We were in the middle of building additional Sunday school rooms.

At the same time, I was dealing with angry members who wanted a different pastor. My marriage was falling apart. I was an officer of the church, but with that constant drain on my energy, I didn't ask God for guidance in my own personal life.

When I went to the pastor with my personal problem, he told me that love is a decision. What did that mean? It didn't help me at all. I was living in a cloud of stress and anger and loneliness. At that point, I didn't want to ask God for guidance because I knew He would tell me to not leave David. I didn't want to hear that. So I stayed away from God.

After I recovered from surgery and gained my strength, I began dating. A year later, October 14, 1982, I married Will. He was a good kisser and a good dancer, and he was charming. I fell in love. I divorced him the following May and remarried him on October 14, one year from the date of our first wedding. Even as I write this I realize how ridiculous that sounds. *What was I thinking?*

Why did I marry him twice? While we were married he was competitive and unkind. After we were divorced, he became the same charmer, only more so, if that was possible. He did everything he could do for me. He courted me. He convinced me things would be different. I believed him and we remarried.

Things were different for a while. Then he became competitive again. When I told him I wanted to quit my job and become a freelance writer, that didn't go over well at all.

My job as assistant director for the Minnesota Association of Townships had become too demanding. I was so stressed I sometimes had to look out the window to remember what season of the year we were in. I knew that if I kept that job I would die young. But Will didn't seem to care about my well being. He could only think about the money. That was a concern for me too. Could we make it financially if I quit my job to write?

I knew if I went out on my own, I would have to prepare beforehand. I had car payments. How much money did we need if we retired? I found that it isn't enough to keep track of expenses for just a month or two and have a clear picture of your needs. But after one year of keeping close track of our expenses, I set up a budget, knowing it would be quite accurate, then paid off my car and began saving money.

My daughters were all grown and living away from home. Laura and Lani were married. I had three granddaughters: Jennifer Nichole Happ, Monica Leigh Happ, and Hannah LaRae Elken. My family was growing. Will was not happy with my future plans. I was not happy with Will. What were God's plans for me? What had I accomplished, and what did I still want to accomplish?

One day I wrote this poem:

A Mother's Worth

A mother searches in her heart
as she examines life.
What has she done except to be
a mother and a wife?

Her other talents dormant -
her children mattered more.
She'd gone to college only after
they were out the door.

But she is feeling satisfied.
Look what she's begun.
The future lies in those four girls.
Her job has been well done.

One took her domesticity,
and creates a happy home
for many children of the world
as well as for her own.

Another used her intellect,
to educate her mind -
added passion to the mix,
and contributes to mankind.

Another took her creativity,
wild and unfurled -
fired it with passion, and
brings beauty to the world.

And one, still youth and loveliness,
she's clay in the Potter's hand.
The canvas for a masterpiece.
God—the keeper of the plan.

This mother's contribution lies
in her four daughters' lives,
as the best of her lives on in them—
improved, magnified, and refined.

This assured me I had accomplished *something*. But I was still at odds with who I had become. I certainly wasn't who Will wanted me to be. What would I become if I didn't follow my heart and become a writer? What else was there for me? What was in my future? What were God's plans for me? I was in contant prayer with God on that issue. *Lord, what do you want me to do?*

CHAPTER FORTY

THE QUILT GOD MADE

Sometimes it's hard to be sure what God is telling you. At least that was how I felt in 1990 when I thought God wanted me to become a freelance writer. But how could I be sure? Keeping track of all my responsibilities at work was like counting cars of a passing freight train. I just couldn't keep up.

I had difficulty getting to sleep at night, worrying whether we could manage financially if I threw security off my shoulders and jumped into untried territory. Will would be retiring soon. We didn't have much set aside for retirement. Was this God's plan or not? How could I know for certain? I prayed for an answer.

In addition to losing sleep over my decision, night after night I tossed and turned, dreaming I was making a quilt. I had purchased fabric and had plans to make a log cabin wall quilt for my office, but the fabric lay on my sewing machine waiting until I could find time to do the project. Every night I made the quilt in my sleep and awoke feeling tired.

I knew I had to find time to make that quilt so it would leave me alone, but my job was demanding. The next week I would be conducting a series of seminars. Monday I awoke with a searing pain in my throat. The more I spoke that day, the worse my throat hurt. On Tuesday morning I awoke with no voice at all. My doctor said, "Stay home and don't even whisper for three days to avoid permanent damage to your vocal cords."

Now I had time to make my quilt. Soon the quilt top was completed. After all, I had made it in my sleep so many times I didn't have to think about how to lay out the pieces. I pinned together the three layers of top, batting, and backing and stood back to admire my work. My groan was almost audible. I had pieced it wrong! It wasn't the design I had planned. I finished the quilt anyway and hung it in my office facing my desk. At least the soft green and mauve creation was pretty and would absorb sound.

The following week my boss decided we should add another series of training seminars to our already hectic schedule. *How could I possibly do more work?* I returned to my desk and dropped my head into my hands. *Lord, I want to quit my job! How can I be sure we will make it financially? I have been preparing, but how can I know it is what you want me to do?*

When I raised my head I stared in surprise at what I had not noticed before—my quilt design formed a large cross that now seemed to radiate and reach out to me. It soothed me and spoke to me, giving me God's promise, "Never will I leave you; never will I forsake you." (Hebrews 13:5 NIV).

It was my answer. I gave my notice the next day, and resigned effective December 31, 1990.

⁓

Will and I had built a retirement home on Lake Mille Lacs near Isle where we moved after I left my job. The plan was for Will to retire too. He was already past retirement age, being sixteen years older than me. But he kept postponing his retirement and I began to work from home as a writer.

Will stayed with his sister Fran during the week while he continued to work. I was my own tough taskmaster, working in my office from eight o'clock to five o'clock every day. I was determined to prove to Will that I could be successful in spite of his belief I would not. My classified ads brought many clients and I was earning money.

I had been attending Metropolitan State University part-time for a few years. In 1991, at the age of fifty, I received a Bachelor of Arts degree in communications. Shortly before that, I left Will. I could not be who I wanted to be and who God wanted me to be while married to Will.

It would take another whole book and more resources than just my memory to adequately analyze my marriage to Will. For starters, I think we both married for the wrong reason and at the wrong time. It had only been a year since Will's wife had died, and only a year since my divorce. We both should have taken more time to learn who we were as individuals before we attempted to become part of a couple again. And we certainly should have learned more about each other before we married. Will clearly was not what I wanted in a husband and I evidently was not what Will expected. Our divorce was final in 1992.

I had turned my back against God's guidance when I left David, and I still had my back turned away from Him in my relationship with Will. How could I expect a marriage to last without God's blessing?

Another granddaughter, Hayley Dee Elken, was born that year. I now had four beautiful granddaughters.

CHAPTER FORTY-ONE

HOME AGAIN

During the ten years I was married to Will, David let everyone know, including me, he still loved me. While I didn't feel love for David, I prayed for him every day. When we were married, he hated to come home to an empty house. "It's so lonely," he'd say. He always wanted me to be there before he got home. So even though we were divorced, I asked God every day to keep David from being lonely.

One day I was getting my hair cut when my hairdresser told me that friends of ours had sold their house quickly. "They are going to live with David until their new house is finished."

"Thank you, God," I whispered. My prayer had been answered.

I had Will and his family, but except for the few months when David was married to Sharon (he asked her to leave less than a year after they were married), he only had our girls. I made it a point to spend holidays with Will's family so the girls would be with their Dad. Although I missed them at those times, I saw them frequently throughout the year.

187

Ironically, David called me in late November, a few days after my decision to leave Will, to inquire what he should buy our daughters for Christmas. He knew I was alone all week, and he had called a few other times with some excuse to talk to me. Several months earlier, he had talked me into coming out to see a farm he wanted to buy. "You have good taste and I want to know if you think I should buy it," he had told me.

So I had met him and his Realtor and had gone out to see the eighty-acre farm. It was a nice location, but I told him the house was horrible. "It should be gutted and remodeled." He bought the farm and moved into it a few months later. Now, when he called about Christmas gifts for the girls, I told him, "I'm going to leave Will."

"All right! When can I come get you?" he almost shouted.

"David, this is not about you. It's about me not being able to live with Will any longer. I'm not coming back to you."

Later in the week, as I made plans to leave Will, David called again and convinced me to meet him at a restaurant. "Just for lunch. Just to talk. No funny business," he said. Since I planned to come into the city that week anyway, I finally agreed.

At lunch, David asked me to come back to him. He promised he would quit drinking and things would be different. He assured me he had never stopped loving me all these eleven years we'd been apart. I said "No." While I could see all David's goodness and was reminded what a fine man he is, I didn't feel any love for him.

The following week David called and begged me to meet him again. "I'll take a day off work and we can meet anywhere you like. I'll come there if you want. I just need to talk to you." I finally relented and agreed to meet him at the same restaurant. We talked about the girls, his family, my mother, and my siblings. It was nice. It felt like old times—the good times in our lives. He asked me to come back to him. Once again, I told him this was not about him. But he did convince me to meet him again the next week to talk more.

During those weeks while Will was gone, I was dividing photographs, linens, dishes, etc., separating our lives one item at a time. I hadn't told Will I was leaving him because I didn't want to deal with the conflict or the "chest pains" he used to try to control me. I just wanted to separate out the material things I had brought to the marriage and leave.

When I met David the next week, we talked about my plans and he said he wanted to help me move. We spent all afternoon talking that day. David had so many plans for us, but I continued to say no, even though I did feel my heart softening after being so hard. Like I was important after being only tolerated. *Was I falling in love again?*

He asked me to come to see the farm again, now that he had moved in. "I want your opinion on what to do with the living room. I'll take a day off work again." I knew it was an excuse to spend more time with me. I could see how much he wanted me back. How much he loved me. *How is it that I am married to a man who doesn't love me, and I keep saying "no" to the one who does?*

Before we parted, he had my promise to come see the farm before Christmas. He gently kissed me on the cheek as we said goodbye. *Did I want to be married to David again?* That wasn't my plan. *But maybe I should re-examine my feelings. What does God want me to do?*

I felt guilty spending time talking with David because, even though I had plans to leave Will, I was still married. "I'm sorry, Lord," I prayed. "Is it wrong to be seeing David? You gave him to me once and I trusted you, but so much went wrong. I threw him away. Do you want us to be together again? Please show me what you want me to do."

I thought about David a lot. I was beginning to feel like the wall I had built up between us was coming down. *When had the wall gone up? I couldn't have feelings for David while I was married to Will. Was that when I put up the wall? Or had it been while we were still married? Had I always loved David and I didn't know it?*

"Love is a decision," came to me like a still small voice. God was speaking to me. They were the words my pastor had said to me.

Those words stayed with me all week. I still didn't understand how that statement worked. One couldn't just love *anyone*. "Show me what you want me to do, Lord." I prayed every day. "I'm so confused."

Toward the end of the week, that same voice whispered, *"To act lovingly is a decision."*

That made sense. Is that what the pastor meant? One can make a decision to *act* lovingly toward someone, no matter how they feel about them? One can open their heart and act with love. I could see that would let down the walls and let the love come in. "But I don't know what that means to me now, Lord. Are you telling me I should go back to David? Surely you don't want me to stay with Will."

Later that week David called with directions to the farm. "If I'm downstairs watching television, I probably won't hear you knock, so just come in."

As I drove toward the farm I began to feel nervous. *What am I doing?* I followed David's directions and drove into the farmyard. I knocked, opened the door, and walked into that same ugly kitchen I remembered. Television sounds came from downstairs so I walked toward the stairway.

"David," I called down. "I'm home!" *Where did those words come from? I hadn't planned to say that!*

David ran up the stairs and took me in his arms. I felt the last walls of resistance fall away, and I realized I *was* home.

"I love you, Connie," David whispered.

"I love you too, David," I said, while I breathed a silent prayer, *"Thank you, Lord."*

CHAPTER FORTY-TWO

ONE STEP FORWARD, TWO STEPS BACK

I moved into David's home and lived with him while I awaited the finalization of my divorce from Will. David stopped drinking for a few weeks. He drank near beer that supposedly has the taste of beer but only a trace amount of alcohol. But all too soon he was drinking real beer again. While I loved David, I was beginning to be more and more frustrated with his drinking. He had assured me, "I won't have to drink if you come back to me." I wanted to believe him, so I did. David is the finest man I have ever met, but his drinking was interfering with our relationship. How soon would we be back to the way we were when I left him? He wasn't hearing me when I told him how concerned I was with his drinking.

Our youngest daughter Cindy was planning a move to Chicago. She asked me to drive there with her and help her get settled. My plan was to stay with her a couple weeks. While I was there I thought a lot about my life with David. I was afraid it would be nothing but more heartache if I stayed with him. I wasn't sure I should go back. I applied for a job with Oprah Winfrey and was hired to work in her office starting the following Monday. Not knowing what final decision I would make about David, for now I was excited about working for Oprah.

The next day, however, I got a call from my sister Donna. Her kidney cancer was back. She needed me in Minnesota. I canceled my exciting job opportunity and packed to leave Chicago. Donna must have told Will that I was in Chicago because he called and begged me to let him come and drive me back to David's. Our divorce was not final and he wanted to talk.

I didn't think it was such a big deal. David did, however. Cindy told him that Will was driving me home and when I got back the next day, David met me on the deck, fury sitting on his face like a physical thing. "You are not welcome here anymore," he spit out. "I've put your clothes and your computer in your car. You can come for the rest of your things later. Your keys are in the car." He turned and walked back into the house.

I stood there in shock. I had just been kicked out of my home! I couldn't believe it. I told Will to wait a minute. I wanted to explain to David that nothing had happened between us and nothing had changed. The door was locked. I knocked, but David wouldn't answer. Will said, "Now maybe you'll come back to me. I love you. Please come back to me." So I followed him in my car back to our home on Mille Lacs Lake. I cried most of the way.

After spending a few days with Will, I knew I wanted to be with David, but I wanted David to be sober. Then Will suggested it would be better if we were apart for a while so our families could better accept our reconciliation. He was throwing me out too. The only belongings I had with me fit into my car. I had little money to rent an apartment or hire someone to move the rest of my belongings. I had always been afraid of ending up like Mom—no money and no security. Now I had become worse off than Mom. I felt betrayed, worthless, and lost.

Without a job, I was fortunate to get an apartment in the same complex where Will and I had lived because they knew me. I began working through a temporary agency. I worked for Dain and Bosworth, General Mills, Arthur Murray Dance Studio, and several other places while I made application for a full-time job. "You are overqualified," I heard over and over again. But I just wanted a job. Any job.

I took the bus to work because I couldn't afford gas and parking. That was a humbling experience as I sometimes sat with winos and homeless people who smelled bad. I was so broke that I bought bread, milk, and cereal at the gas station because I could use my credit card. Credit cards were not yet accepted at grocery stores. I tried to adjust my working hours so I could drive Donna to her chemotherapy appointments.

I developed a frozen shoulder and had to have surgery and then physical therapy. The therapist told me she wasn't surprised I had a frozen shoulder because I carried the weight of worry on my shoulders. I felt bereft. I felt forsaken. I was in deep grief over Donna. I felt betrayed by David and betrayed by Will, the two men who professed to love me.

I was in a dark pit where I didn't think my Heavenly Father could see me. I didn't call out to Him. Yet God continued to speak to me through dreams. I was like King Nebuchadnezzar of biblical times who knew his dreams were important, but couldn't understand their meaning. I kept a diary of my dreams, and as I read them now, I can see that God was repeatedly trying to show me I needed to let go of the control I was so desperately hanging on to and give my life to Him. But I couldn't see that then.

Instead, I felt lost, but I didn't know how to be found. I kept trying to hold my life together. Will called, but I didn't want to see him. I prayed for guidance regarding David. I missed him, and I knew in my heart that I belonged with David. But David wasn't calling me. I worked wherever I could in order to pay the rent and put gas in my car. My life consisted of working and visiting

Donna, and I was digging myself deeper and deeper into a dark, sorrowful place.

One day I was out of toilet tissue at home and had no money to buy more. As I used the restroom at a gas station, I was tempted to put that extra roll of toilet tissue in my purse and walk out with it. But I couldn't do that. I couldn't steal. I had promised God long ago that I wouldn't. Instead I wadded up a bunch of the tissue and put that in my purse. I thought God would forgive me for that small indiscretion. I was stooping lower and lower. At Christmas time I looked through my belongings and found things I could give my children and grandchildren. I had no money to buy gifts. I realized how easy it was to become a person who lived in her car.

I was one paycheck away from being homeless.

CHAPTER FORTY-THREE

DONNA

He wasn't her usual doctor that day in late August 1992. He looked more like a patient than a renowned specialist, his tired eyes peering deeply into Donna's pain before he extended his hand to me and said, "You're Donna's sister." He didn't expect a response.

A few questions from him—a few questions from her—all with his face buried gravely in her voluminous file. Another handshake and he shuffled out again, shoulders stooped. No cancer-curative vials to take home this time. We did well, smiling blindly at the nurses as we left.

The big flat rock beckoned to us, warm and sunny, between the clinic door and my smoke-free car. We sat down. Fear gnawed holes in my soul as I sat there shivering, thinking about tomorrow's sorrow. Donna smoked one whole cigarette in silence, and then lit up another.

"He did say 'weeks,' didn't he?" she finally asked.

"They don't know for sure," I said. "You could have more time than that." I couldn't cry unless she did. That was her rule.

"My birthday is in ten weeks."

"I know." *Only forty-eight.*

"I wanted at least another year."

"Me too."

She lifted her chin and blew smoke into the beautiful Minnesota morning. "There's so much I want to do yet."

"I know."

We sat there while she inhaled deeply, exhaled, inhaled again. She smoked slowly and deliberately, savoring—savoring that cigarette as if it was her very life.

Then she gazed into the distance and asked. "What kind of person am I?"

"Oh, Donna, don't you know?" I said. "Don't you know how special you are? Don't you know how much we all love you? You're a great mother, a loving wife, generous daughter, and the best sister in the world. You're a wonderful person," I assured her.

Then it dawned on me. *She's finally allowing the question.* "Are you ready to meet your maker?" I asked softly.

Her tears came in great, gulping sobs, granting me permission to soothe my own hot, raw, throat. We cried and held each other—in public, in the middle of the day. Finally she straightened up, blew her nose, and said, "Well, I haven't been good all my life."

I explained that it doesn't matter, that God loves her and sent his son to die for her sins so she could go to heaven. "I know all that," she said. "But what do I have to do *now* to make sure I'll go to heaven?"

I led Donna in a prayer confessing that she believed Jesus Christ was the only son of God and that she knew she was a sinner who could not save herself. She asked forgiveness for her sins and invited the Lord to come into her life that day on the warm, sunny rock—then smoked another cigarette. On the way back to her apartment I took the wrong turn somewhere and headed in the opposite direction, but Donna said I was allowed. We each had the Jenny Joseph *When I Get Old I Shall Wear Purple* poster on our walls, allowing us to act outrageously. We had decided to "wear purple" now, since she was never going to get old.

She got worse. No longer able to handle the stairs, hardly able to answer the door, she met me one day in a purple sweat suit, red hat, and a brandy snifter in her gloved hand. She thought *I* needed a good laugh. And she never blamed me for not dying first because I'm older.

The New Year arrived. The dust collected on my shelves as she grew thinner every day when I went to see her in the nursing home after work. My own sister, but I couldn't help, except to keep her company—and share my life—because she no longer had one, confined to the nursing home at forty-eight, blessed only by her ninety-eight-year-old roommate's deafness, her privacy nonexistent, her "things" crowded into half a closet and the top two drawers of a small bureau … makeup, an address book, cards … and a few candy bars stuffed into the night stand, all comforts of home a lingering and yearning memory seldom mentioned in our discussions as I sat with her, talking, while my laundry piled higher and the sink filled with dirty cereal bowls from morning and another from evening when I returned home to cry again.

Today her legs were more swollen. Today she breathed with more difficulty as she sat at the smoking table, smoking one cigarette after another. What did it matter now? Her tumors grew in her huge white belly, and her thin chest and arms looked like holocaust photos, and her head—angular, with teeth too large— and I loved her so much.

I brought her yarn so she could knit one more memory for her daughter and I pulled too-tight elastic out of her waistbands. I bought her new lipstick and mascara and offered to help her write last letters but she said they were too personal, she would do it herself, but I knew she wouldn't—because she couldn't.

She said she wanted to go home to sort through her belongings—give things to people who could use them. "Our feet are the same size and I have lots of good shoes," she said. "Laura could use my books on ceramics." But she fell asleep during meals, and her feet turned purple, and she didn't mention her apartment again.

One day I said, "Donna, I love you so much. I will never forget you."

"You better not," she said. "Or I'll wake you up during the night with the rattle of a stick against a rail fence."

My mail sat in stacks, unopened, in my apartment. I remembered to pay my rent. Donna scolded me when I forgot she couldn't drink ice water, and got angry because I asked a minister to call on her. I filed and polished her fingernails. She saw the man sitting in the corner again—the man no one else could see.

In February my sister Rennie (Irene) came from Arizona and asked why I still had my Christmas cards displayed. When I forgot to offer her hangers, she found a place in the coat closet for her things. I cut up a towel so we would have clean washcloths. We ordered pizza. When she needed a safety pin, I remembered one had been lying on my bedroom floor for several days—maybe weeks. I was grateful that she loved me.

They said Donna called out for me Sunday night, but I had gone home to sleep and they didn't call me, and when I got there the next morning she could no longer speak and I'll never know what she wanted to say to me—or what she needed me to say to her. Her eyes just implored me silently—then returned to sweet escape of sleep while I read to her of God's unending love.

She died at four o'clock in the morning on Tuesday, March 2, 1993. In that quiet pre-dawn hour, the man that only she could see must have stood and walked to her bedside saying, "Donna, it's time to go." I know she reached out with a radiant smile to our Dad, who went before her fifteen years earlier. I can see her rise from her wretched body and go hand-in-hand with him through the tunnel of light to heaven.

The funeral was over. Everyone went home. I looked in the mirror and saw Donna's eyes in my face, and tears for her suffering and pain became tears for my own loneliness. I knew Donna was in a better place now, with no more pain, but I missed her.

The sound of a stick against a rail fence woke me at four o'clock one morning and I knew it was Donna. It made me smile to know that I will see her again some day.

I also know that when it's my time to go, Donna will come to meet me, and because she always was just a little bit outrageous, she will be wearing purple.

CHAPTER FORTY-FOUR

WALKING PARTNER

David attended Donna's funeral. It was the beginning of our reconciliation. He consoled me during the service and we talked alone for a while afterward. "I'm sorry about letting Will drive me back from Chicago," I told him. "I was confused and frightened by the fact that you were still drinking, and Will wanted me to come back to him. I thought I needed to hear what he had to say, and it was a way for me to get home, so I agreed to let him come and drive me. Nothing happened between us. I don't want to be married to Will, David. I want to be married to you. I love you."

We continued to see each other for a few weeks and I continued to pray about my decision to go back to David. During those weeks, God continued to give me dreams that, when I analyzed what they meant, always seemed to tell me that my home was with David.

David finally forgave me, and we were remarried after my divorce was final. On June 4, 1993, I was one of the happiest brides to say, "I do." This time I had remembered to bring God into our plans. I could almost hear God telling me that He gave

THRIFT STORE SHOES

David to me long time ago and it was about time I recognized how fortunate I was. Needless to say, our daughters were happy to see their parents back together again.

Before I went to Chicago, we had torn down walls in the farm house, put in doors, stripped, sanded, painted, wallpapered, and shopped for appliances. The major portion of the house had been remodeled. Now I was going back to the house with a new blessing upon us as a married couple once again. We began restoration of the rest of the farm as if we had never stopped. We pruned old shrubbery, raked, planned, walked down the pasture lane, poked around in the barn, and fixed fence. So much to do. But I was eager to work with David to restore this farm to beauty. I attended a landscape design class and created a master plan to implement as we had time and money.

The winter of 1993 was full of new adjustments for me—a new marriage, a new home, a new community, and a new church family. I loved it all, but I needed a walking partner. That's what I was telling the neighbor I had invited over for coffee, but she was too busy talking to listen to what I was saying. *Oh well,* I thought, *God will find me a walking partner soon.*

I had been praying for a walking partner for several weeks. I needed the exercise since I sat in my home office writing all day. I enjoyed walking, but being a city girl, I was afraid to walk alone in the country. David was too busy to walk with me when he came home from work, but he assured me it was safe to walk alone during the day. "I know I probably shouldn't be afraid, Lord," I prayed, "but I feel frightened alone on the empty stretches of roadway. Please find me a walking partner." While I waited for His answer, I occasionally drove into town and walked where I felt safe.

When the spring community education catalog arrived in the mail listing a Power Walk Workshop, I knew God had answered

201

my prayer. Surely I would meet someone there who could become my walking partner.

When it was my turn to introduce myself at the workshop, I said I was new to the community and was looking for a walking partner. After class a young woman said I was welcome to join her and her friends at the high school each afternoon at four thirty. But that was when David returned home from work and I wanted to be home then. A middle-aged couple invited me to walk in the evenings with them, but they lived about seven miles from me. I also did not want to walk with the women who went out at six thirty because I do my best writing first thing in the morning. I preferred walking later in the day when I need a break from my keyboard.

"Okay, Lord," I prayed, "I know I'm particular about where and when I walk, but surely there is someone near me who wants to walk when I want to walk." I met several people at church and introduced myself to my neighbors. But still no walking partner.

The weather was getting warm and many days I just wanted to walk out my driveway and down the road a bit. But I had another problem. I couldn't get our big German shepherd to stay home when I tried to go for a walk, and I didn't want to be pulled around by a big dog on a leash.

I didn't know much about dogs, except my heart had gone out to this one when David found the brandy-colored puppy sniffing our garbage cans that past winter. He was skinny, shivering with cold, and so frightened he hardly dared accept our hospitality at first. "Sounds like another country drop-off," the woman at the animal shelter said when we called. "We'll keep the information on file, but it's not likely anyone is looking for him. He probably got too big for the owners to handle." He was certainly at that awkward stage, but his sad brown eyes melted my heart.

We bought a small bag of dog food and placed an ad in the local paper describing the lost dog. We bought another small bag of dog food. Then another. By then Brandy returned all the affection we gave him, and he became my constant companion. The day David came home with a twenty-pound bag of dog food, I knew Brandy was here to stay. But now he was big and uncontrollable, and my attempts at training were completely ineffective. I had successfully raised four daughters, but I had no idea how to train a dog to obey me.

I found a dog obedience class and enrolled us. Brandy proved intelligent and eager to please. I soon had him leash trained to heel, sit, stay, and come. One day after I put the choke chain on him for our daily training sessions, I decided to try walking down the road with him. It went pretty well. We did it again the next day. And the day after that. Brandy enjoyed exploring the countryside as much as I did.

After walking with him on the third day, I removed his choke chain, patted him approvingly, and said, "Thanks for the nice walk, Brandy. You are a good little walking partner." And then it hit me. *Walking partner!*

Of course! All these months while I asked God repeatedly for a walking partner, He had already provided one. My Father knows me so well. He sent me a walking partner that would be eager to go walking with me *whenever* I wanted to go and *wherever* I wanted to go. And I would certainly be safe with a big German shepherd at my side.

One day a few neighbor dogs came into our yard and spirited Brandy away to our neighbors who raised chickens. The dogs, Brandy included, raided the chicken house and killed the chickens.

Dave and I had both learned that once dogs get a taste of killing chickens, they don't stop. We had to find a different home for Brandy. I felt sad to lose my wonderful walking partner, but I thanked God for the ideal companion He had given me, and the lesson to look around and see if God has already answered our prayer before we keep asking.

CHAPTER FORTY-FIVE

LOOKING FOR REWARDS

I worked as a freelance writer from my home office, and David and I had an agreement. I'm a city girl and I was not going to become a farmhand. Yet there he stood, asking me to come out and help bale hay.

"I'm not the farmer in the family," I told him, turning my attention back to the computer. "I don't know how to drive a tractor and bale hay. Can't you find someone to help you who knows how to do it?"

David stood at my office doorway in his John Deere cap, short-sleeved chambray shirt, blue jeans, and work boots, trying his best to entice me out of my air-conditioned office into the hot, humid field. "I don't know how to drive a tractor," I said once again.

"I'll show you how. It's easy," he repeated.

I glared at him.

"I can't find anyone else to help me. It'll only take a few hours," he coaxed. "Give it a try, honey, just once. Okay?"

I can dig in the dirt with the best of them and I love gardening, but this was different. This was farm work. If I learn to drive a tractor, what will he expect me to do next?

I glanced at my computer screen, then back at him. He evidently sensed a crack in my resistance because he bounded into my office, lifted me from the chair, and walked me out with a smile that seemed to acknowledge an assent I didn't remember giving. "I don't want to do this," I said. But he was already telling me to put on a long-sleeved shirt and my wide-brimmed garden hat, and to wear my leather garden gloves. Before I knew what hit me I was sitting on a tall green tractor trying to follow David's instructions on how to shift the craziest gear system I'd ever seen.

I didn't know what a fifty-five-year-old grandmother was doing on a tractor when it was ninety-five degrees out. I searched for the right gear, let out the clutch slowly, and looked back at David standing on the hay wagon hitched to the baler that was hitched to the tractor. *I'm supposed to drive a whole caravan of machinery?* David was smiling from ear to ear as he waved me forward. *He better appreciate what I am doing for him!*

By the time we made a few rounds, I was able to keep the tractor tire at the edge of the windrow so the baler tines picked up all the hay and I could make the turns correctly. Since I couldn't hear David's voice over the noise of the machinery, he whistled whenever he needed my attention. When he whistled, I'd look back and he'd direct me to shift to another gear, adjust the speed, or stop so he could make a tension adjustment on the twine-tying mechanism. Every time I looked at him he was smiling. Our dog, Freddie, a bluetick/heeler cross, ran back and forth alongside us and was having a great time. Well, at least *they* are both happy, I thought.

We went around and around the field, the baler fingers feeding the hay into its noisy mouth and pulsating a compact, oblong bale of hay out the other end, one chug at a time. Dave's slim, muscular body leaned forward and pierced each bale with a sinister-looking metal hook, pulled the bale onto the wagon, then carried it to the back of the wagon and stacked it five or six bales high. He definitely had the hardest job, but I didn't give in and smile at him.

When I faced forward again I saw a young doe right alongside our path. I looked back at David and he nodded that he saw her. She calmly grazed on leftover strands of hay and looked at us nonchalantly while she chewed. We went around the field several times with our chugging machinery passing close enough to allow us a good, clear look at her before she disappeared back into the woods. Freddie trotted alongside us on the opposite side of the tractor, pouncing on frogs, oblivious to the deer standing so close.

When we finished baling that afternoon, David thanked me profusely. I was glad he appreciated my help, but I felt God had already rewarded me by sending the deer to visit us.

"Not again!" I grumbled a few weeks later when it was time to bale the second cutting. I now knew what I was doing, but it still wasn't what I *wanted* to be doing.

"Come on, honey," David said. "It wasn't so bad, was it?"

This time, as we chugged around the field with me at the controls of the 2510 John Deere tractor, pulling the New Holland baler that was something from the sixties and a hay wagon that had seen better days, I thought about my office project not getting done. *I deserve something for sacrificing my own valuable time for David's pursuits.* Sure enough, brilliant flashes of blue from the wings of a pair of bluebirds feeding near the line fence delighted me over and over. Once again, God had given me the reward I thought I deserved for haying.

When it was time for the third and final cutting in late summer, I begrudgingly went out again, but I was now on watch for the reward I knew God had for me. Around and around the field we went, but there were no signs of deer, or bluebirds, or eagles, or anything wonderful—just Freddie running back and forth with us until I worried for his well being. He chased birds, ran after snakes, dug for gophers, and pounced on frogs. But he never strayed far from us. When David called for him to jump on the wagon and rest, he obeyed, but all too soon he jumped down and began running again. He occasionally shared a drink of water from our thermos, then ran ahead of the tractor, leading us around the field. A couple times he lay down in a shady spot on the edge of the field to cool off for a couple minutes, but he never let us out of his sight, or allowed us to get too far away.

That day was particularly beautiful. The late summer sun was warm, but not hot. The sky was a pretty blue with no clouds in sight, and a mild breeze caressed my face with the warm smell of new hay. I felt a wonderful sense of relaxation and well being. *Okay, this isn't what I chose to be doing out here on the farm, but maybe all farming jobs aren't unpleasant.*

As I continued to watch Freddie, his commitment to us, to being near us at all times, amazed me. I couldn't believe his dedication to staying with us for hours, running at our side or ahead of us as if it was his job to care for us. He made me feel unconditionally loved and protected. *Just like God does,* I thought. God is always near us, guiding us, protecting us, and loving us. And Freddie was a gift from God after we lost our last dog—a reward, just as the deer and the bluebirds were rewards.

That made me wonder how many other rewards I overlook every day. Do I forget to appreciate all that I have, starting with my loving, patient husband? I get wonderful rewards of being able to live on eighty acres of unspoiled countryside and to enjoy, daily, all the wonderful wildlife it sustains. David and I both are blessed with the ability to earn an income at home. We have our health. I thought of our children, their families, brothers and sisters, and my mother. I thought of so many good friends and neighbors we enjoy.

I finished the last windrow and pulled back the power takeoff lever to stop the baler mechanisms. I looked back at David and the huge load of hay bales. He smiled his always-ready smile, gave me a thumbs-up, then gestured to "take us home."

I smiled back at him, returned a "thumbs up" and blew him a kiss. I realized I need to be more on the giving end of the reward system and learn to be more thankful for the rewards I get daily.

And maybe being a farmhand once in a while isn't all that bad.

CHAPTER FORTY-SIX

A WRITING LIFE

Dave retired from Northern States Power Company on December 31, 1993, after working thirty-one years as a lineman and line crew foreman. I continued to write. My first published story appeared in *Evangel* magazine in 1993 as a two-part story. Needless to say, I will always be grateful to Vera Bethel, the editor who published that story.

I enjoyed the freedom and flexibility of writing from home, doing what I wanted to do, when I wanted to do it, where I wanted to do it. Many others asked, "How can I have the same freedom and flexibility? How did you do it?" Eventually, after enough people asked me, I described the process in a book.

I wrote *Quit Your Job and Make Ends Meet,* but was unable to find a publisher willing to publish it. I didn't have the credentials. I wasn't a financial planner or psychologist. It didn't matter that I wrote from my own experience.

In 1994, I attended a three-day *Artist's Way* seminar by Julia Cameron. That Bethel College auditorium was filled with people who wanted to change their job situation so they could do what they wanted to do. The air was filled with a fog of frustration and desire to make changes in their lives.

I had the answer for them. The world needed what I had to say. I could not wait for a publisher, so I self-published my book. I borrowed six thousand dollars and had twelve hundred books printed.

I began marketing my book by setting up interviews with newspapers, radio, and television. I scheduled fifteen classes through local community education that fall based on my book. I was able to repay my loan that first year. I continued teaching classes throughout the state for five years, long after all the books had been sold.

It was the week between Christmas and New Year's Day, 1995, a time when I usually clean my office and plan for the next year. What should I write next? As usual, I talked to my Heavenly Father about it, asking His guidance. Strong thoughts came to me: *organize your photographs.*

Silly thought. I didn't want to organize my photographs. I had boxes of them. The last thing I wanted to do was spend time sorting through them, putting them in albums.

That still, small voice came again: *organize your photographs.* No, I don't want to organize my photographs. Why am I thinking about this? "Lord, I want to write something else. What should I write?"

Organize your photographs. This time the thought was so strong it was almost an audible voice. I realized God was speaking to me. But why does God want me to organize my photographs? Am I going to die and He wants me to have photos organized for my family?

"Okay, Lord," I said. "I'll do it."

That began a long tedious job of going through many boxes of photographs, sorting them by chronological order, and putting them in albums. I was struck by the fact that I had lots of photos of Mom's family, but hardly any of Dad or his family. Why didn't

I have photos of Dad's family? I hardly knew any of them. I had heard stories about how Dad's father had left and the county took the children away from their mother, and how Dad was raised by an uncle. But I suddenly had a strong desire to know more.

I called Dad's sister Cora in California, the one child Dad's mother had raised, and asked if I could come visit her and talk about family. She was delighted to have me visit.

I spent two weeks with Aunt Cora at her little house in the country in the San Bernardino Valley where she lived alone. Except for a couple car trips, we spent all our time talking about family. We watched no television. We didn't listen to radio. We didn't read any newspapers. She told me all about her mother and father and the tragedy that happened to them. Her mother had told her how the judge took her children away on a trumped up charge, and how she knew that a wealthy couple had adopted her youngest boys, presumably for money under the table for the judge. She tried to tell her older brothers that, but they wouldn't believe her.

Two weeks later, I walked into the house, happy to be home, as one always is no matter how wonderful the trip has been. On the kitchen table lay that day's newspaper, with the front-page headline in big letters—OKLAHOMA BOMBING. Large photos of the disaster were printed under the headline. I felt as if I had been punched in the stomach!

I reluctantly read the article. After such peace and quiet with Aunt Cora for two weeks, this news was almost more than my psyche could handle. Then David turned on the television. The noise sounded horrible to me. The same with the radio. It took several days for me to acclimate myself to the influx of media we are faced with each day in our lives. I hadn't realized what a difference it makes on our physical bodies and our mental state of being. Certainly it is not to our betterment.

I began writing my grandmother's story. I wanted to exonerate her, now that I had learned the truth. But did Aunt Cora really know the truth? I needed more information, so I went to the Wright

County courthouse in search of records that would confirm what Aunt Cora told me.

With the help of one of the judges I had worked for, we found Ella Ingram Duncan's court records in the musty sub-basement of the courthouse. They substantiated Aunt Cora's story and more. I photocopied everything and wished with all my heart my father had known the truth. If he had known his mother did love him and she wanted him so very much, it would have made a difference in his life, in my mother's life, and even in my life.

That year, my first grandson Ryder Lounsbury Fedyk was born. I taught forty-two more workshops based on my book, and I wrote the first draft of my novel *Kathleen Creek,* based on the story of my grandmother's tragic life. I realized God had wanted me to organize my photographs because He knew it would lead to writing this book. It has been a work of love. While I have been published many, many times—both books and short stories—I still have not found a publisher for *Kathleen Creek.* Did God want me to write something I felt passionately about so I would continue to write and learn more about writing? Or does He want me to get it published? Maybe, until recently when I changed it to Christian historical fiction, it wasn't the book he wanted published. No matter what, I have no doubt that God led me to write this book. God willing, it will be published some day.

In 1996, I taught twenty-eight more *Quit Your Job* workshops, and my interest in flowers led me to become a student of floral design. David built a gazebo for me and my flower gardens flourished under almost constant care. Gardening is a jealous lover. It demanded too much of my time, but I loved it.

In 1997 I continued to teach *Quit Your Job* classes and received certification as a Master Gardener after completing specialized horticulture training. In 1998 another granddaughter, Kathryn Emmaline Ford was born.

CHAPTER FORTY-SEVEN

TAKING CARE OF MOM

I wanted Mom to come live with us after her stroke in 1998, so why was I feeling so angry about having her here? What was wrong with me? I didn't like feeling this anger. To make it worse, I didn't know who or what I was angry with. I wasn't angry with Mom. I didn't blame her for not wanting to live in a nursing home after her stroke. She was only seventy-eight. She couldn't live alone any longer, but when we showed her a nice assisted living facility she cried as if she were heartbroken. Mom deserved better than that. David and I were both home all day. It made perfect sense that Mom come live with us and I take care of her. But then I felt angry so much of the time.

Every morning I awoke in our dark basement bedroom and the first thing I thought was, *Is Mom okay?* I climbed the stairs and Mom was already sitting at the kitchen table, her walker at her side. She didn't sleep well; neither did I. I felt groggy. My eyelids were puffy. I sleep best with open windows. Mom kept the windows closed in our former bedroom where she slept, and we slept in a basement bedroom with no windows at all. Mom was always so cold that we kept the house much too warm for our comfort. I wanted my own cool bedroom back! Anger crept in and I felt ungrateful. "Lord, forgive my selfishness. Mom deserves the best we have to give her. Forgive me for my anger," I prayed often.

Mom had lived a hard life. She never had anything nice. After we children grew up and moved away from home, Mom slowly began accumulating a few comforts. Then Dad died, leaving no money and no life insurance. Mom found a cleaning job at a nursing home within walking distance from her apartment.

Now Mom was sick and elderly. She had taken care of us children all those years, doing everything the hard way. She deserved to be cared for with all the comforts we could give her. We brought some of her furniture to our home and made it her home too. For months I maintained a steady schedule of doctor's appointments and therapy sessions to overcome the effects of her stroke. Most of the time Mom didn't feel up to any kind of socializing. She didn't want visitors. She tired easily and couldn't remember the words she wanted to say. We installed a separate phone line for her so she would feel comfortable to call her friends at any time. When I finally invited people over, she became upset with me. Why did she always have to be so difficult? We had a life too!

Although our farmhouse was small, we converted our own bedroom off the kitchen for Mom, installing a television jack so she could watch television in her bedroom, in her favorite chair, if she wished. "I can't get any of my shows on this television," she complained.

"We can't get cable this far in the country yet, Mom," I told her.

She continued to whine, "There's nothing on TV." I stopped what I was doing and played cards with her.

We bought another recliner chair for the living room and rearranged our furniture so she could be comfortable reading in a sunny spot or watching television with us. "I can't see to read anymore," she said. I went to the library and checked out large

print books for her. Then she said she couldn't read because she
was so dizzy. I took her back to the doctor again, then to the
pharmacy for her new prescription. I felt like the only thing I ever
did was go to doctors. Why didn't my sisters come and do some
of these things? Why did I have to do it all? We installed safety
handles in our bathroom so she wouldn't slip and fall, but I still
had to help her in and out of the tub. Just when I thought one thing
was taken care of, something else went wrong with her.

I tried to get some of my own work done, but Mom wanted to
talk, so we talked. I loved my lifestyle before Mom came to live
with us. With our daughters grown and gone, and David outdoors
all day caring for cattle, raising crops, or fixing farm machinery, I
had quiet days to write. Now I hadn't written for several months. If
I did get into my office, I kept wondering if Mom needed anything,
or I was listening to whether she was okay, or I was trying to think
over the loud voices of Festus or Matlock. My sisters were still
earning an income from *their* jobs, but I could no longer do *my*
job. Just because I worked freelance didn't mean I didn't work or
didn't need the money from my work. I began feeling angry again.
The anger started from my toes, filled my whole body, and erupted
like horns sticking out of my head. I hated myself when I felt this
way. I prayed, *"Lord, help me to be a better person."*

As Mom recovered her speech and motor skills, I began a
series of appointments with her to further improve her quality of
life. She needed cataract surgeries in both eyes, and she needed
new hearing aids. I thought she would want to watch television
and visit with others when she could see better and hear better
again, but that didn't happen.

I felt like I was slowly reverting to my childhood, when
positive thinking was a foreign concept. I had moved beyond all
that, but now I was living with Mom's negativity again. She would
rather complain about her pain than take medication to alleviate
it. She wouldn't even listen when her therapist tried to show her
how to use my can opener. It was different and she hated it. My

impatience with her was turning to ugly anger. How could I be angry with Mom? *It must be frustrating when her body doesn't keep up with her spirit of wanting to be whole and healthy. Lord, help me to be patient.*

My impatience and anger with Mom was beginning to spill over into other areas of my life. Someone from church called and asked if I would help with the pictorial directory again. *Don't I have enough to do already?* A niece called and asked if we could have a family reunion at our farm because we have such a nice large area? *And who has time to do all that?* My daughter called to see if her two teenagers could spend Tuesdays and Thursdays with us for the summer while she works. *Don't I have enough responsibility already?* Where was all that defensiveness coming from? My anger was a rat inside me, eating holes in my soul. I was so ashamed of myself.

I had registered for an evening class, and David implored me to cancel. "You know I don't want to be alone with your mother," he told me as I hushed him so Mom wouldn't hear. "What if she has another stroke?"

"I need some time for me," I whispered. "I have given up all my other activities since Mom came here. I need to do this, David. Please try to understand." Talking quietly through clenched teeth, my throat, neck, and chest felt tight and hard and angry. Tears fell hot on my face, the anger draining my energy again. I retreated into my office and cried. When I finally reached for a tissue, my eyes fell on the typed Bible verse I keep taped to the wall, "I can do everything through him who gives me strength." (Philippians 4:13 NIV).

Even this, Lord? Even my inability to cope with Mom living here? How?

"I'm going for a walk," I called to Mom and David as I grabbed my jacket and headed toward the road. I began praying, "Dear God, please take away this anger. Take away this anger and replace it with strength. Take away this anger and replace it with joy. Take away this anger and replace it with love. Take away this anger and replace it with patience. Take away this anger and replace it with kindness. Take away this anger and replace it with consideration. Take away this anger and replace it with understanding."

As I walked and cried and prayed this prayer I began to feel a peace come into my heart. I got to the main highway and turned back. Starting from the beginning, I prayed again that my anger be replaced by every good quality I had been lacking since Mom came to live with us. By the time I got home I felt stronger. *I can do everything ...*

The next week I found myself praying that prayer many times every day. When Mom wouldn't even try to dress herself like the occupational therapist had shown her, I prayed, "Please, God, take away my anger and replace it with patience." I could feel the anger leaving, and then I could say lovingly to Mom, "Let me help you. Now, how did Thelma say you should put on your blouse?" When Mom said, "I don't need my hair washed. We're just going to the clinic," I felt the anger returning. "God, please take away my anger and replace it with kindness." Then I could say with a smile, "Mom, I haven't washed your hair for several days. It will only take a few minutes and you'll look so nice."

Eventually I discovered that my anger had been replaced with a better attitude, a softer heart, and the strength to deal with the difficulty of caring for my mother. Without that anger draining my energy, I found time to go for short walks with her, to take her to town, and even go to the city on outings we both enjoyed. I still wasn't finding much time to write, but when I did write she was always interested in what I was writing. She encouraged me. Soon I found she was there to share my joys and successes. She was there to console me when I had a concern or some bad news. We talked about her childhood and I learned more about my own heritage. As I talked about God in my life, she shared with me that even though she didn't attend church and was not one to talk openly about her faith, she had a personal relationship with God and she prayed frequently.

Eventually Mom was less difficult to live with, but she missed the city lights, the noises of the city, and being close to her friends. She was now capable of living somewhat on her own, so even though my sister Rennie would be at her job during weekdays, Mom wanted to move to the city with Rennie.

After Mom moved out I was comforted in the knowledge that Mom was prepared to go live with God. I now have many memories of being closer to Mom, and I know that it is possible for God to take away my faults when I am willing to work on them myself along with Him.

Shortly before her eightieth birthday, my mother got pneumonia. She was on a ventilator and kept so heavily sedated that we couldn't communicate with her. Dave, my sisters, and I spent seven days in the hospital with her, and then she was gone. I knew Mom had gone to a better place and that she had no more pain or sorrow, but my mind was full of regret that we didn't get to say goodbye to each other.

Every morning that spring and summer while Mom lived with us she had said, "Well, we better go see what's new in your flower garden today."

Mom loved the huge, vibrant, orange oriental poppies that waved in the wind. They reminded her of the crepe paper flowers we kids used to make in grade school and bring home to her. She pointed to my columbine and talked about how she had sucked the honey from wild honeysuckle as a child. When my peonies blossomed, the fragrance jogged memories of my father who had died years before. She talked about how much he had loved peonies, about the peonies that had grown next to the white metal fence of his childhood home, and about the peonies Dad had planted at two of their homes.

My lilacs reminded Mom of the farm where she grew up, and my hollyhocks were a reminder of her mother's pink hollyhocks that grew against the rough gray siding of her childhood home. My garden was always a trip down memory lane for Mom. It became our best times together as she reminisced.

While we sat and admired the flowers, I told her how much I appreciate the Monarch butterflies that I call "flying flowers." "The Monarchs are a faithful butterfly," I told Mom. "They migrate all the way to Mexico in the fall and return here to their breeding ground the following spring. Many people believe they represent the miraculous transformation our bodies make when we enter heaven."

Mom tried to get a closer look at the black and orange beauties, but they always flew away before she could get close. When I tried taking a close-up photograph, they eluded close inspection by me as well. Mom would say, "There go your flying flowers again."

Now, after Mom's funeral arrangements were made, and David and I drove back into our farmyard, I saw the September splendor of my garden. My heart ached with grief that Mom would never sit with me in my garden again.

We knew that my brother and his family from Colorado would be arriving at our home any minute. When I walked into the house, even through my tears, I could see the kitchen floor needed sweeping. I picked up the entry rug and went out on the deck to shake it. David was still outside. As I turned to go back into the house he called my name. "You have a butterfly on your head," he said.

I turned and looked at my reflection in the glass of the door. A beautiful Monarch butterfly was sitting right on top of my head. "Wow!" I said. "In all my years of gardening, a butterfly has never landed on me."

I continued to look at our reflection and I felt a warm sensation. I said, "Is that you, Mom? Are you telling me you have made the miraculous transformation and that you are safe and happy in heaven now?" The butterfly moved her wings up and down slightly. Fresh tears sprung to my eyes. *Yes,* I thought, *Mom has no more pain and no more loneliness. I shouldn't be sad. She is in a far better place, I know.*

I turned my head from side to side. The butterfly stayed in place. I walked across the deck to my husband. "I know this butterfly is a message from God. But I can't believe it is staying there so long."

He looked at me and said, "It's still there, all right."

I walked back to the glass door and looked at it again. The butterfly just sat there looking at me. I stood there for the longest time, watching and listening to the silence. I walked across the deck again. "I don't know why it doesn't fly away," I told David.

"He seems to like being there," he said.

I walked back to our reflection. The butterfly looked back at me. "Thank you, God," I said. "Is there anything else you want me to know?" Ecclesiastes 3:1–2 came to mind—*There is a time for everything, and a season for every activity under heaven: A time to be born and a time to die.* (NIV) The butterfly seemed to look straight at me for a few seconds, and then she gently flapped her wings and flew away. As I watched her leave, I knew Mom was waving a loving goodbye to me.

I eased into a deck chair and felt the warm wonder that replaced the heaviness I had felt earlier. God had sent a Monarch butterfly to bring me a final visit and a fond farewell from Mom. And, obviously remembering my frequent prayer to Him, "Lord, please speak to me clearly so I will understand you," He spoke to me in a message He knew I would understand.

CHAPTER FORTY-EIGHT

TEARS

It was a gray, drizzling day and I was suffering from the kind of late spring cold that made me feel unjustly put upon. Why now, after I had survived the Minnesota winter and all its accompanying colds and flu? It wasn't fair! The ringing telephone interrupted the nap I was trying to take.

"This is Little Mountain Flowers," said the feminine voice. "We have a delivery for Connie. I'm just calling to make sure someone will be home."

"I'm home," came my nasal response.

Why am I getting flowers? I wondered. *My birthday is still three weeks away.* Fear gripped me momentarily as I wondered if I had forgotten our wedding anniversary. But I quickly realized that was more than a week away. Had I done something especially nice for someone recently? I couldn't recall that I had. I had been sick with this cold, but not sick enough to warrant flowers. Hmmm?

I put the kettle on for a cup of green tea (isn't green tea supposed to be good for colds?) and asked David, "Are you sending me flowers?"

"Not this time," he said.

By the time the tea was cool enough to sip, our dog Freddie announced a visitor and a woman handed me a clear vase filled with a beautiful fresh bouquet. A dash of sunshine on a cloudy day! *They do such nice work at Little Mountain Flowers,* I thought, my eyes feasting on the orange roses, deep pink asters, and yellow heliopsis. Deep purple tulips not yet ready to release their smiles were tucked in among spikes of curly willow and deep glossy greens. A yellow, orange, and pink plaid ribbon around the neck of the vase echoed the flowers' colors. But who had sent them?

I slipped the card from its envelope and read, *Now it is my turn to carry on the tradition. I love you, Mom. Lisa*

It took a few seconds to understand what my daughter meant. Then, memories of my mother hit me like a blast of air from a passing semi truck. I burst into tears. My mother had died two years earlier and last June Lisa had called me on my birthday. I was feeling sad because I had always given my mother flowers on my birthday to thank her for my life. I could no longer do that. Today was Lisa's birthday, and she was sending me flowers. *Her turn to carry on the tradition.*

Thoughts of my mother turned to thoughts of Lisa and her expression of love for me. Unexpected and undeserved. How could I ever tell her how much this meant to me? Had my mother felt like this every year when she got my flowers of appreciation? I hope so. She wasn't good at expressing her feelings. But here I am, a writer—a wordsmith—and I could find no words to express my overwhelming sense of being loved. I could only cry.

It is what others do that they wouldn't have to do, or be expected to do, that means the most. *Like the ultimate gift of love when Jesus died on the cross for our sins.* Those words came rushing into my mind like a flood. *Unexpected. Undeserved. That is why you cry.*

That was the answer to my often-asked question, "Why do I cry when we sing songs of praise in church?" There are no words to express the overwhelming sense of being loved that I feel during worship. So I cry, to my embarrassment.

But now I felt God was telling me that it is okay to cry to express my appreciation to Him, just as it is okay to cry with joy at my daughter's love for me. Crying is another form of communication. And it is okay.

CHAPTER FORTY-NINE

THE REAL ME

"I'm too sick to get dressed," I told David when he came in from warming the car against the Minnesota cold. He didn't argue. He just helped me put my winter coat over my nightgown and robe, and held my arm as we embraced the dawn of Sunday, December 23, 2001.

Our small-town hospital emergency room doctor asked, "How long have you been sick, Connie?"

"Two days," I answered.

"Do you smoke?"

"No."

"Have you ever had surgery?"

I don't know. Why can't I remember? "David, have I?" I asked him.

They took my temperature, checked my blood pressure, listened to my lungs, drew blood, did an EKG, and took chest x-rays. My eyelids wouldn't stay open. I heard, "We're going to put in an IV now, Connie," and I moaned at a sharp needle prick. "Connie, this is oxygen to help you breathe," someone said as they put plastic tubing into my nostrils and wound it around my ears.

Then, "Connie, we're going to admit you to the hospital. You have pneumonia in both lungs."

Pneumonia! Just like Mom. Two years ago, also on a holiday weekend, we had brought my mother to this same emergency room thinking she may have had a heart attack or another stroke. I can still hear the doctor saying, "Good news. It's pneumonia. We can cure that." Seven days later Mom died.

Same hospital. Same doctor. Same diagnosis. *Lord, make me well.*

I was patterned after my mother. Same body shape, same baby-fine hair, sensitive skin, and nearsighted eyes. Same allergies and lactose intolerance. But this wasn't the same. Mom was almost eighty. She had smoked all her life and had suffered a stroke. I was sixty. I had never smoked, and I was strong and healthy. God would answer my prayers and make me well.

That day I slept between blood pressure checks, changes of antibiotics on my IV pole, checking my temperature, and checking my oxygen level. My temperature had soared to 104.4 degrees, my oxygen level had dipped to 85 percent, and they were watching my blood pressure very closely because it was hovering around 78 over 50.

Our parish nurse came to see me. When she looked at the antibiotics I was getting, she said, "These are the strongest antibiotics available." Yet, they weren't helping. I was beginning to be very concerned about my condition. When my primary care physician came in that morning she had said, "This was your mother's room. Did you remember that?" I hadn't, and it did nothing to comfort me. Mom died from her pneumonia. *Would I die? Lord, make me well.*

My room was dark except for the light coming in from the hallway. Nurses had been coming in and out of my room all day and night, and as I lay there with my eyes closed, I heard another nurse come quietly into the room to stand at my bedside. I opened my eyes. No one was there. *That was strange. I know I had heard someone.* Soon I heard the same distinct sound of quiet footsteps coming softly into my room to stand on the opposite side of my bed. When I opened my eyes, again no one was there. *Am I hallucinating? I know I heard footsteps.* A little later the same soft footsteps came and stopped at the foot of my bed. Yet no one was there. Then I heard a soft flutter above my head and realized there must be a vent overhead where all those sounds were coming from. I went to sleep.

Later during the night when a nurse came in I asked her to help me to the bathroom. I put on my glasses, since I can't see far without them. As I was going back to bed, something outside my window caught my eye. An angel was suspended outside my window! The angel glowed in the darkness of the night. I realized God had sent an angel to watch over me.

As I lay in bed marveling at the angel, I realized that the footsteps I had heard earlier that surrounded me were angels sent by God to protect me. *Thank you, Lord!* I am sure I fell asleep with a smile on my face because I felt enveloped in God's love and protection. I was assured that I was in His hands!

The next morning I looked out my window to see if the angel was still there. I only saw a street light. *Had it been the light of a street lamp that I thought was an angel?* As I studied it carefully, I could see a vague shape of an angel. But it had appeared so very much like an angel during the night. Perhaps God shaped the glow to look like an angel even more so I would realize He had placed angels around my bed for protection. He had wanted me to feel His presence—to be comforted. But I had not recognized His attempts to alert me to His actions by allowing me to hear the footsteps. He had to give me something else so I would hear His message and be comforted.

The antibiotics were not helping, and x-rays showed my lungs were filling fast. My fevers kept spiking, and I awoke frequently drenched in sweat. Respiratory technicians came in four times a day to give me nebulizer treatments and lower the head of my bed, then pummel my back and sides. They were trying to break up the pneumonia because I wasn't coughing. My body became sore from the assaults. Each new shift nurse seemed surprised when she first listened to my lungs. "Sounds like Rice Krispies. Snap, crackle, pop."

"This is the worst case of pneumonia I have seen," the doctor said. I was able to provide a small sputum sample and the culture showed no influenza. "You're not responding to treatment," she said. *Those were the exact words she had said to Mom.*

Even in the vagueness of my medicated mind, I realized too many coincidences were happening. *Is the Lord trying to tell me something? What message am I supposed to hear?*

Mom came here on a holiday weekend, had pneumonia, stayed in this very same bed, was transferred to North Memorial Hospital and put on a respirator, and died. I came here on a holiday weekend with pneumonia, and am in the very bed Mom was in. *What am I supposed to understand from this?*

Mom was never in control of things. I loved my mother, but I spent most of my life trying to be unlike her. She accepted poverty without trying to change things. Mom delegated most of the home management to me. I had learned how to put enough fillers in a pound of hamburger to feed a family of seven, and how to patch pants, darn socks, turn collars, and find enough denim left in a pair of worn-out pants to make a child's coat. I learned a fistful of wild flowers on the kitchen table will draw one's eye away from the black, worn spot on the linoleum floor, and that privacy is possible when sleeping three-to-a-bed if you learn to cry silently. I learned to take control and make things better. I had accepted Christ into my life, and now I knew God would make me well because I asked Him to make me well.

But my condition worsened. I was too sick to care that I missed Christmas. The doctor ordered a CAT scan of my lungs. Still perplexed, she said, "We have not ruled out transferring you to North Memorial Hospital in case you need to be intubated."

That's what they did to Mom! The ambulance crew had swept into Mom's room, lifted her onto a cart, and whisked her into the ambulance. Running to keep up, I had followed in my own car. Once there, they put Mom on a respirator where she developed complications. We stayed at the hospital with her day and night until they turned off the respirator. She died immediately.

Now I realized that I too might die. Was God telling me that I should prepare for that eventuality? *Is that why all the parallels with Mom?*

My first thought was of David. We haven't had enough time together yet this second time around. We are still trying to make up for those twelve years we were divorced. *Lord, I don't want to leave David again. Make me well.*

After eight years of remarriage, David and I love each other more than ever and treasure every day we have together. We never look back.

We never look back! That thought hit me like a bright light switched on after sitting in a dark room. *We never looked back.* That's how I was able to blame David for our divorce, even though *I* was the one who left *him.* That jolt put a mirror before me I had avoided facing for twenty years. All my faults that led to our breakup mocked me.

I tried to put them out of my mind by thinking about David. David, who couldn't commit to anyone else all those years because he still loved me. David, who cries when I cry. David, who thinks I am beautiful, even though I have become old and gray and undeserving of a man who sees me through such rose-colored glasses.

The mirror wouldn't go away. I was forced to face myself. Married at barely seventeen, I had three children before I was twenty-one. With little time or money, the few times I was in a social situation without a baby on my lap I became flirtatious when we did go out on occasion. I thought it was harmless, but it hurt David. When I went to work as a waitress a few evenings a week while David cared for the children, his anxiety increased.

I went back to school and earned a degree and the ability to work in a law firm. David was afraid the well-dressed men with whom I worked looked better to me than he looked, coming home in dirty work clothes. By that time he was drinking, and no matter how much I assured him he was wrong, it fell on deaf ears.

Our own social life had become nil because of David's jealousy, so I started going out after work with coworkers, both men and women. Again, I told myself that it was harmless, but it drove David deeper into the bottom of a bottle of beer.

Soon we had nothing to talk about except the children, who, all but the youngest, were grown and gone. A house without love is lonely. I took our youngest daughter and left.

I needed someone to love, and found a man who sopped up my affection like a dry sponge. We got married. When I had refused to return to David, he also remarried. "I need someone," he told me.

David's marriage didn't even last a year. Mine lasted ten. But God brought me back to David after my disobedience. I didn't deserve him anymore than I deserved the grace God gave me every day of my life.

The doctor came in, interrupting my thoughts. "Your blood pressure is very low. If it goes any lower we'll have to put you on dopamine, a very strong medication. We would need to monitor you carefully, so we would move you into intensive care. We'll just keep a close watch for a while yet."

I don't want to go on this medication! Lord, please keep me off this medication.

I realized what I was saying. I was asking God for what *I* wanted. I wasn't trusting God to do with my life what *He* wanted. I was still trying to control everything instead of turning my life over to God, like I should have done before I left David.

I wanted to live, but I suddenly realized that maybe God wanted to take me home now. Was I ready to accept God's will? No. I didn't want to die yet. Not yet. I needed more time. My daughters still needed me. I wanted to see all my grandchildren grow up. I wanted more time with David. I couldn't die yet!

But if God wanted to take me home now, was I ready? I searched my heart and my soul as tears flowed freely onto my pillow. *Do I need to forgive anyone?* I couldn't think of anyone. Do I need to ask forgiveness from anyone? *Yes. First God and then both men whom I divorced, especially David.*

Although David and I were happy, it was bittersweet to think of the years we wasted and what could have been. But perhaps without the interruption of our life together, we may never have appreciated our time together now as much as we do. I know now that when God chose my life partner when I was still but a child, He knew what He was doing. It was me who forgot to trust Him in all things. God gives us consequences when we are disobedient, much like the Israelites who were forced to walk the desert for forty years. So now I must live with the consequences of my disobedience. Was He taking me home without having enough time with David?

I continued to cry, searching my heart, readying my soul. Finally I prayed, "Lord, thank you for giving David back to me, even though I don't deserve him. Please forgive my sins and take me to heaven when I die. And Lord, if you want to take me home now, I am ready. I put my life in your hands to do with as you wish. In Jesus' name, amen."

Tears continued to flow like a shower cleansing my soul while a nurse came in and took my blood pressure, patting my arm in an attempt to comfort me. She left with tears in her own eyes.

Our pastor, Jim Tetlie, came to see me then. He tried to comfort me. He prayed with me. He assisted me in filling out the Living Will I wanted to have on file. I didn't want David to have to make the kind of decision we had to make about taking Mom off the respirator.

I had read of great peace people feel just before they die. Now, after pastor Tetlie left, that wonderful sense of calm I had read about replaced the anxiety I had been feeling. It made me feel certain I *was* going to die. I lay in bed waiting for what was next. I whispered, "It's all up to you now, God."

How foolish of me! I thought. It had *always* been up to God. I had been trying to control God with my prayers, believing I deserved to live because I was a good Christian and because I asked God to favor me with life.

Surely, God wanted me to see myself for who I am, to ask forgiveness, to give up control, and trust Him with all aspects of my life.

I get it, Lord. I finally get it. I remembered Second Corinthians 12:9: *My grace is sufficient for you, for my power is made perfect in your weakness.* (NIV)

I had stopped crying when the nurse came in again with the blood pressure monitor. "Wonderful!" she said. "It's up just a little. Maybe you won't have to go on dopamine."

That was the turning point in my recovery. My blood pressure slowly continued to climb. My temperature eventually returned to normal. They took out my IV.

A male nurse steadied me as we walked across the hall to the shower where he bathed me and washed my hair while I sat on the shower stool without embarrassment—only gratitude to him for doing what I was too weak to do for myself.

My appetite improved and I regained strength to walk on my own again. But the parallels with my mother's life continued. On her seventh day after entering the hospital, my mother went home to live with the Lord. On my seventh day after entering the hospital, I went home to my beloved David—humble, grateful, and determined to trust God with my life.

It was as if God was saying with a wink, "Don't forget what you've learned now, Connie."

I hope I never do.

CHAPTER FIFTY

BLUEPRINT FOR SUCCESS

For five years I taught adults how to get out of debt and live on less income through community education classes around the state. These classes were based on my book, *Quit Your Job and Make Ends Meet*. My students included mothers who wanted to raise their own children, people who wanted to start their own business, early retirees, and others who couldn't make ends meet. Many were mired in heavy consumer debt. Our society's "buy now, pay later" philosophy had paralyzed their attempts to reach financial and lifestyle goals.

The students paid a modest sum for the class, but I spent numerous follow-up hours helping some of them fine-tune budgets, contact creditors, or start a home-based business. My biggest challenge was inspiring them to believe they *could* turn their financial picture around. Many were in despair of ever being anything other than broke.

Then I met Robert.

While I was visiting a friend in Duluth, Minnesota, we were invited to a party hosted by Mickey Paulucci, owner of Grandma's Restaurants, at his fabulous home on Lake Superior. Guests came from all over the world. Even the chef flew in from Switzerland. Huge yellow and white striped awnings graced the vast green lawn. The three hundred dinner guests sat at long tables covered with crisp white linen cloths. Here was the world of wealth and prosperity my students aspired to but believed they could never attain.

Robert, the young man who sat across from me at dinner, was obviously wealthy. His rings glittered, and a wide gold chain around his neck shone richly against his shiny black skin. He was so personable I felt comfortable asking about his life. He graciously told me his story.

He was born into a large family in Jamaica. Like many families in that country, they were extremely poor. Robert's parents insisted their children go to school every day, do their homework every night, and attend Sunday school every Sunday. As they walked barefoot to Sunday school, each child carried two bags. One bag held their clean shoes and stockings and the other a wet cloth. When they neared the church, they stopped at some bushes, washed their dusty feet with the wet cloth, and put on their shoes and stockings. They tucked the bags under bushes, and then walked into church clean and properly dressed. After church they reversed the process and walked home barefoot again. They did this, of course, so the shoes and stockings would not wear out too quickly. They had to be passed down from child to child as they grew.

Robert wanted his own business some day. He knew that America is the land of opportunity, so he planned to come to the United States when he finished high school. He worked and saved money, and one day he was ready to leave Jamaica. Before he left, his mother said, "Robert, I know you will be successful in America because you have everything it takes to become successful."

Robert thought about what little money he had in his pocket and asked, "What do I have?"

"You have ambition," she said. "You have determination. And you have good manners, because your father and I taught you good manners. You have a God who loves you. That is all you need. You will be very successful."

Robert came to Miami with his mother's words written on his heart. He bought an old, used Ford automobile and found a job as a doorman at a large hotel. His mother was right. Good manners earned him good tips. Each day when his shift at the hotel was over, he changed out of the regal red uniform, got into his car, and went to a local pub where he had become acquainted with several other young men. They drank a couple beers, ate dinner, and played a few games of pool. When they all left to go home, Robert got into his car and began looking for a place to park for the night. You see—Robert slept in his car.

Robert didn't want to spend his money on rent, utilities, and furniture. He was determined to own his own business as soon as possible. He ate most of his meals at the hotel. He washed his few clothes at a Laundromat, and he put every dollar he didn't spend into the bank.

The day finally came when Robert was able to walk into a car dealership and pay cash for a long, white, stretch limousine. He quit his job at the hotel and started a limo service. Then he moved to the high-rent district. He now slept in a limousine.

Robert earned good money with his limousine business. His manners continued to serve him well as they brought repeat customers and good tips. He was able to save even faster than before. This time it didn't take as long before he was able pay cash for another limousine.

Robert hired a driver for his second limousine. Then he rented an apartment and moved in. Now he had a street address and all the collateral he needed to go to the bank and borrow money for more limousines.

Robert handed me his business card. It read *Transportation Fleet.* "Oh," I said. "You have a whole fleet of limos now!"

"Yes," he said. "And trucks. And buses."

"You really have been successful," I said.

"God has blessed me abundantly," he said. "In fact, my business was recently featured in *Entrepreneur* magazine as one of the best young companies. We netted a profit of 10 million dollars this past year."

"Congratulations. How old are you Robert?" I asked.

He smiled. "I just turned thirty-five."

Robert said he has never forgotten where he came from. He regularly goes into the inner city and tries to show minority children they *can* escape the ghetto and make something of themselves. What an inspiring young man!

After that, I always concluded my classes with Robert's story. Occasionally I heard "Wow!" But mostly the students just got up from their seats and silently filed out of the room, lost in thought. Later I heard how Robert's story had inspired many of them to make changes in their spending and savings plans.

God puts the right people in our path at the right time. That evening Robert was the right person to be seated across from me at dinner. He not only inspired my students, he inspired me as well. I began prioritizing and saving my *time* as Robert had prioritized and saved his *money*. That afforded me the time I needed to write the novel I wanted to write.

I hope I will always remember that lesson I learned from Robert.

CHAPTER FIFTY-ONE

GOD CHANGED MY HEART

Many years ago, I attended a weekend seminar for goal-setting. During that weekend, we were asked to write a one-sentence lifetime mission statement. My statement became: *My mission is to help others to be the best they can be.* Since then, whether in my everyday life, my work, or my volunteering, I've tried to remember to ask myself if what I am doing fits with my mission in life. That led to volunteering to teach adult literacy. After a couple years of doing that, I switched to volunteering as a mediator for Anoka County. I wanted to diffuse some of the frustration and angst in the world.

I was mediating with a lot of divorced parents regarding child custody and visitation, and a lot of angry, frustrated people. I wanted so badly to counsel them, but that is not what mediation is about. Mediation is helping the parties find a way to compromise and agree on a solution to their *immediate* problem. I wasn't allowed to bring up the subject of church or faith or God. That left me feeling frustrated, wanting to do more for them. I wanted to follow them out the door and say, "Let me tell you what might help you."

I had the desire to be a counselor when I was in high school, I wanted to counsel divorce clients when I worked as a paralegal, and now I wanted to counsel my mediation clients. Evidently God wanted me to become a counselor. That is not the path I chose, however. But because I needed to be able to tell people about God, I moved into a different area of volunteering.

I felt God's call to prison ministry long ago, but I dragged my heels. Hebrews 13:3 reads: *Remember those in prison as if you were their fellow prisoner, and those who are mistreated as if you yourselves were suffering.* (NIV) The call felt heavy upon me. Yet I said, "I'm too busy." "The prisons are too far away." "My husband doesn't want me to go." When I heard about *Charis*, I asked what their volunteers do. The answer was, "In a nutshell, we go into state and federal prisons and just love the inmates."

I couldn't do that. Would the man who raped my cousin be there? How about the man who traumatized my niece as he robbed the bank where she worked? How could I love them?

One day I was reading Matthew in the Bible. In chapter 25:36 Jesus says, *"I was sick and you looked after me, I was in prison and you came to visit me."* Verse 39 states, *"When did we see you sick or in prison and go to visit you?"* Jesus answers in verse 40, *"...whatever you did for the least of these brothers of mine, you did for me."* (NIV)

The call was too strong. I became a *Charis* volunteer. Imagine my surprise when I walked into the prison chapel expecting to see a bunch of criminals, but instead saw a room full of pleasant men who were extremely grateful for our visit. Despite their crimes, they showed goodness as I became acquainted with them.

Genuine love filled my heart each month I visited and worshiped with them. I shared God's love with them and gave them hope and encouragement so as to better endure their suffering. In return I learned more about God in our discussions and my faith deepened. God loved me enough to change my heart and make me a loving person.

After serving as a volunteer for *Charis* for three years, I began to find it difficult to drive safely at night. It's a two-hour drive one way to the prison. I didn't want to leave *Charis*, as I had made many wonderful friends there, and I knew I would miss the inmates if I didn't see them each month. "How can I leave them, Lord?" I prayed. "Those visits are important to them and to me."

I agonized for several months and spoke to the volunteer coordinator about my dilemma. "Maybe you could volunteer for the PVS program instead," she told me. I learned that the national Prisoner Visitation and Support Program is volunteers who go into federal or military prisons once a month and visit with three or four inmates for an hour each one-on-one.

I also learned that the Federal Correctional Institution that I visit, with over 1,400 inmates, had only *two* volunteers visiting there on the PVS program. "The list for inmates wanting visitors is very long," the volunteer coordinator told me. I would be able to drive there in the daylight and still get home before dark. That sounded perfect to me.

I began the paperwork to be admitted as a PVS volunteer. "I only have one request," I stated in my application. "I don't want to visit with inmates charged with crimes against women or children."

I was eager for my first visit to meet the three inmates assigned to me who were at the top of the list. Most of them had been waiting for three or more years for a visitor. The first two, a Hispanic man and a Native American, were pleasant to visit with and expressed deep appreciation for my visit. We discussed their families, what they liked to do, their jobs at the prison, etc. One of them told me that coming out of the crazy prison atmosphere into the quiet, peaceful visiting room with all the different colors, and visiting with me, felt a little like freedom. The other inmate told me, "When a stranger like you cares enough to come and visit me here, it gives me hope that society will accept me when I get back home."

The third inmate, a white man, told me he was convicted of buying child pornography. He had only bought it out of curiosity. He said he avoids other inmates, hoping they won't learn of his crime, as he had been assaulted by other inmates, in another facility, when they learned why he was there. He was depressed and said he used to be a good person. People were proud of him and liked to be with him. Now he doesn't even know who he is anymore.

I couldn't help wondering how much of what he was telling me was the truth. Convicts are often good con men. If he was really a victim of circumstances and tough sentencing guidelines, as he claimed, why did he get such a long sentence? Why would he want to watch such horrible crimes against children if he wasn't a monster himself?

His depressed state of mind made it difficult to visit with him. He needed someone to give him hope. I tried to cheer him up, but I wondered whether I did want to visit him again.

Should I continue to visit him? Why was I given that inmate to visit? Those questions weighed on my mind every day. I had to make a decision before the next month's visiting day.

That Sunday my pastor talked about how one sin is as bad as the next sin. He referred to the Samaritan woman at the well that Jesus spoke with. I had read and heard that story many times, but this time the story spoke more directly to me. The pastor repeated that it didn't matter to Jesus that she was a sinner, a social outcast. He loved her anyway. Jesus called her a "special lady." He treated her with dignity. "And that is how we are to treat all sinners."

I knew God had spoken to me through pastor Jim. I would continue visiting with this depressed inmate who has no hope for his future. He is a sinner, and it doesn't matter what his sin is, I will treat him with dignity and try to give him some hope.

And, maybe, just maybe, God chose this man for me to visit so I could learn to not judge others. Romans 2:1 says, *You, therefore have no excuse, you who pass judgment on someone else, for at whatever point you judge another, you are condemning yourself, because you who pass judgment do the same things.* (NIV)

The Hispanic inmate I had been visiting was transferred to a camp closer to his family, so I was assigned to a different inmate to visit. This older man told me he is in for bank robbery. This man did not look like a bank robber. But what does a bank robber look like? He had robbed the bank for drug money. He had been incarcerated for three years and had not had a visitor during that time. He was delighted to come into the visiting room and have someone to talk with. And talk, he did. When he learned that I would come and visit him every month, I thought he was going to weep.

As of late 2011, the U.S. Bureau of Prisons housed 210,177 inmates. PVS had a total of only 315 volunteers throughout the United States who go into these facilities to visit inmates.

Most federal and military prison in the United States has a long list of inmates who have requested a PVS visitor, and most of them have no, or few, other visitors. They committed crimes and they need to serve their time. But they also need to see goodness in the world to which they will someday return. I believe the kindness of visits can contribute to less recidivism after release.

I strongly encourage others to consider PVS, headquartered in Philadelphia, as a volunteer opportunity.

CHAPTER FIFTY-TWO

FAMILY

In high school, my brother Lee played the guitar and joined his second cousin Donnie Ingram and a couple other guys to form a band. They played on weekends at the Eagle Lake Pavilion. What fun! I danced with anyone who would dance with me. We danced the twist, jitterbug, and slow dances. Lee played a lot of Johnny Cash songs. I especially liked "I Walk the Line." "Blue Suede Shoes" was one of my favorite Elvis Presley songs. But my favorite of all was when Lee played "Wildwood Flower" on the guitar. I could listen to that all day. And to think—my own brother was making such beautiful music!

One of my fondest memories of Lee is riding with him in his 1947 red convertible with the top down. He bought that car for ninety-nine dollars when he was only seventeen. Like me, Lee always had an after-school and weekend job during the school years and worked full-time during the summers. He worked at Merwin Drug at Lyndale and Broadway as a dishwasher and soda jerk. He worked for Klier's Nursery and Garden Center unloading boxcars. He worked for Bachman's Garden Center driving truck. He worked for a sod farm rolling up and loading sod. Dad had a

1948 Jeep with a snow blower on the back, and Lee helped Dad blow snow. He mowed lawns in the summer.

Lee studied tool and die making on the work program at Minneapolis Vocational School. He graduated in 1959, enlisted in the Air Force shortly thereafter, and served two years. He was married and had two sons. In 1965, he fell doing steel construction work and became a quadriplegic. He and his wife divorced.

Even paralyzed from the chest down, he made a productive life for himself. He married Aurora, a woman who worked at Craig Rehabilitation Hospital in Denver where Lee was nicknamed "Super Quad." They adopted a beautiful daughter Anjelee. Lee patented a valuable invention to assist wheelchair-bound people and has helped others through ham radio operating. He makes wonderful scroll saw plaques and wall hangings, maintains a vegetable garden at their home in Denver each summer, and has been an inspiration to his family and to all who know him. At seventy-two, he continues to defy statistics about the survival rate of quads. He is still my hero.

I was blessed with three sisters. While I felt more like a mother to my three younger sisters while we were growing up, as adults I treasure them as close sisters and confidantes. The older we get, the dearer they become to me. I feel bad for women who have no sisters.

Donna, only three years younger than me, was only forty-eight when she died. It was at a time in our lives when our children were pretty much grown, but still quite young, especially hers. She and her husband owned a restaurant, and the only way to see her during her last few years was to go to the restaurant and hope she had time to sit at a table with us and visit for a while.

After she died, my other sisters and I realized we didn't spend enough time together. It was a wake-up call to our own mortality. We set up a plan to, at the very minimum, spend a sister weekend together once a year. Since we each live in different states, some years that was all we got.

Eventually the weekends began to grow into many days together after Rennie began earning good money. Because she knew that Judie and I could not afford much travel, Rennie funded many trips by car and by motor coach, and even a Mexican Riviera cruise. In response to our thanks, she only said, "I want to spend time with you and I can afford it, so it's okay."

We have been so blessed by, and I am so grateful for, her vast generosity. To be able to travel with my sisters has allowed me to see the country I otherwise would not have seen. And seeing the country is one of my greatest joys. I am not a tourist—I am a traveler. I want to see what Mother Nature created in our wonderful world, not what Walt Disney created. I want to eat where the locals eat; I want to meet the people; I want to hear their music and see their homes.

Traveling is not high on David's priority list. He would usually rather stay home. We have had a few great trips together in our pickup camper, including a trip to Alaska, but unless David has his home on his back, like a turtle, it is not David's idea of fun. So I do most of my traveling with my sisters.

All the fun things we sisters have done together have been wonderful adventure. But the best part of being together is still the talking time. Girl talk, we call it, but it is the nourishing of our souls as we remember the past, discuss the present, and plan the future.

Now that we all live in different states—Lee in Colorado, Rennie in California, Judie in Iowa and me in Minnesota—we still try to get together as often as possible. Judie and I meet halfway between us twice a year to celebrate our birthdays. I try to visit Lee as often as possible, and Rennie and I usually see each other at least once a year.

I am so rich in family with my amazing brother and my awesome sisters. We also have many cousins and a few aunts and uncles left, so reunions are a lot of fun.

I received a huge blessing recently in that I met my Uncle Clifford (you can read about him in my up-coming novel *Kathleen Creek*) who is ninety-one years old. He had been unjustly taken from his mother when he was two and adopted by another family. My dad, who was twelve at the time, died at sixty-five and never saw his brother again. A tragic story. But God brought Uncle Clifford back to us in a wonderful reunion. I also met his son and his wife who live here in Minnesota. I know we will see more of them and keep in contact. Family ties are so important.

All our four daughters and their families living within an hour from our home. They are all blessings to us. Their spouses make up for never having had any sons. Jack O'Connell Ford, born April 20, 2000; and Emily Addison Ford, born November 28, 2001, complete our list of eight grandchildren. We also have a great-grandson, Ashton Jordan Aasen, born February 2, 2006. Needless to say, we have a very long dinner table on Thanksgiving Day, and much for which to thank my Heavenly Father.

Family is one of God's greatest blessings.

CHAPTER FIFTY-THREE

TURNING A NEW PAGE

On June 14, 2011, I turned seventy years old. As I approached that date, I realized I had reached "old" and began to feel a sense of anticipation. Much as Donna and I had once agreed to "wear purple" when we got old, the dawn of this new decade brought a sense of freedom and daring. I began asking God, "What shall I write on this new page of my life?"

Recently I was in the middle of a Bible study class at church ... I don't remember exactly what was being said ... when a thought entered my mind very clearly, "*Tell* people how to hear God's voice."

I got so excited about this idea that I could hardly concentrate on the rest of the Bible study. *Was God really calling me to speak on such a grand theological topic as How to Hear God's Voice?* Was I equipped to speak on that topic? I remembered that God does not call the equipped, He equips the called. *But was He really calling me into a speaking ministry?*

About the same time this occurred, I was reading through decades of my personal journals in case I might be reminded of something to add to this book. Shortly after I heard God speak to me about telling people how to hear God's voice, I read my journal entry dated June 12, 1989. I was married to Will at the time. I read

When I found The Helper by Catherine Marshall, I felt as if it was a gentle reminder from God that I should write. Catherine has been my heroine for many years. She is truly an instrument of the Lord. I want to be used as she was. As I read this book, Catherine is once again helping me. But there is still one major unanswered question, "How do you really know when God is speaking to you?"

Wow! God spoke to me again! He was showing me there is a need for someone to go out and answer the question that I once had—that I know so many people have.

I wrote that in my journal in 1989—twenty-two years ago! Why has it taken so long for me to learn how to hear God's voice, and to be ready to be used as I wanted to do?

It was because I needed to know the Bible better. I needed to know God better. I wasn't ready. God knew that. How difficult it must have been for God to watch me struggle to grow without knowing how. I wanted God to use me, but I was untrained for the job. Why didn't I turn to the Bible sooner? For a woman who believes she is intelligent, I certainly have exhibited a lot of ignorance.

On June 15 of that same year, I wrote in my journal: *I am still reading The Helper and praying for the Holy Spirit to fill me, leaving no room for Satan. I pray, "God, change me, make me worthy, then use me." I pray for the answer to, "How do I know for sure what God wants of me? How do I know when He answers my prayers? How can I hear Him?"*

Now, I felt as if God was calling upon me to answer that question for others. Do I know enough now to do that? As I look back in this book to the many times God has spoken to me, I realize that I have learned how God speaks to us. He has spoken to me in various ways. Is that enough? Can I do what God is asking of me? I felt unsure—fearful.

Then I read what I had written a couple weeks later, on July 4 of that same year:

Our guests at the lake over the long weekend left, and I lay on the bed reading from Catherine Marshall's A Closer Walk. Then I napped. I dreamed I was in the sky and I could stay there without support. But as I lay there, I began to be afraid of moving, in case I would fall. To test it, I somersaulted in the air. I came back right side up and I was fine.

Upon awakening, I believed God was telling me I can do unbelievable things if I have faith. I must overcome my fear—He will keep me safe. I must dare to venture beyond the "safe and secure."

Now, while I write this book, God is speaking to me through these dreams once again. Yes, He gave me that dream years ago when I was struggling with the decision of whether to quit my job and become a writer. But now He was telling me, again, that I must overcome my fear. He will keep me safe. I should dare to venture beyond the "safe and secure." I could become a speaker.

After that dream in 1989, it had been additional assurance from my Heavenly Father that I could resign my position as Assistant Director of the Minnesota Association of Townships and become a freelance writer. So a year and a half later, I did. We moved our belongings to our new home at Mille Lacs Lake and I started my freelance writing business Communication Spectrum. It has been a successful, satisfying career move.

In 2001, I won First Place in the inspirational category of the *Writer's Digest* Writing Competition for my short story, *Coming Home,* the story about Harold and his dog Teddy. I was awarded seven hundred dollars in cash and one hundred dollars in *Writer's Digest* books, my name was published in the *Writer's Digest* magazine, and that story was published in the winners' booklet. Submissions to that category numbered 1,900.

Over the years, I have received many writing awards, and my short stories have been published in many books and magazines in the United States and Japan. I have taught writing classes through community education in several school districts, and I have spoken at various events. I edit for other writers and have ghostwritten other people's books.

The book that I co-wrote with Deanna Germain, *Reaching Past the Wire: A Nurse at Abu Ghraib*, was published in 2007 by Borealis Books, an imprint of Minnesota Historical Press. It is Deanna's memoir about her experience caring for the Iraqi prisoners at the Abu Ghraib Prison Hospital.

Writing is a labor of love. For most of us, it doesn't pay all the bills. I try to not compare myself with other writers and only pray that my books and stories be published in order to honor God.

The books on my shelf that have not yet found a publisher include the Christian historical novel, *Kathleen Creek*; a post-Vietnam Christian novel, *Yellow Curtains*; an authentic collection of inspirational Civil War letters and diaries entitled *Phineas Sylvester Rudolph, A Civil War Love Story*; a young reader novella entitled *Deer Story*; and a children's book called *Hunter Bear*.

I also have enough true inspirational stories for a book. And I keep writing more, because I must. It's what I do. It's what I love to do. It's what God wants me to do.

Now the same messages I heard from God years earlier are speaking to me again, telling me to dare to venture further and begin a speaking ministry. I have spoken a few times on, "How God Speaks to Ordinary People," and it has been well received. I love hearing how it helped people. I know God is speaking through me, and I am honored to be doing that.

I know for certain it was God telling me to start a speaking ministry. How do I know that? First, because the idea came to me during a time when my mind and heart were open to receiving His word. Second, because the thought came to me clearly like a still, small voice. Third, because I became excited about it, and I have maintained that excitement. I have a sense of peace about it. That is God telling me that He wants me to do what I am doing.

Another way I know for certain God was speaking to me was when He gave me the same message by more than one method. After my initial nudge by that still, small voice, the following Sunday our pastor's sermon clearly told me I need to speak to people about hearing God's voice. Then I read those old journals and heard myself as an uninformed Christian pleading with God for answers, and agonizing because I didn't know how to hear Him. It told me how important it is to learn how to hear God speaking to us. Then my cousin Terry Hasse brought Stonecroft Ministries to my attention. So I am in the process of getting approved to be a Stonecroft Ministries speaker.

I may be at the dawn of my December, but I am privileged to be an instrument of God's words and wishes as long as He keeps me around. I know that He will continue to give me the words to say and the courage to say them. After all, the Bible states in Matthew 10:19, *"Do not worry about what to say or how to say it. At that time, you will be given what to say, for it will not be you speaking, but the spirit of your father speaking through you."* (NIV)

And I know that in the process of teaching others, I will learn more and will grow even closer to my Heavenly Father. Like Michelangelo, who was 87 when he said, "Ancora imparo," I am still learning!

CHAPTER FIFTY-FOUR

FINAL PROOF

From the time I changed careers to become a writer in 1990, I wanted to write for *Guideposts* magazine. Dr. Norman Vincent Peale and his wife Ruth started *Guideposts* in 1945. It's an international inspirational magazine with a readership that numbers around six million people. They publish true stories that inspire people. I believed God wanted me to write for Him. It would be the epitome of my career if I could write for *Guideposts*.

Every two years *Guideposts* has a writer's contest. Out of thousands of entries, the editors choose only fifteen winners. I sent a submission to the contest in 1992, 1994, and 1996 with no luck. I also kept sending them stories. They kept sending them back. Eventually they did publish two of my stories. One of the editors told me it is unusual to be published in *Guideposts* if you are not one of their family of writers.

"How do you become one of their writers?" I asked.

"You have to win the writers contest and be trained by *Guideposts* editors." So I knew I just *had* to win the 1998 contest.

But 1998 was the year my mother had a stroke and came to live with us. I knew the contest deadline was looming, but I hadn't had time to look for a story because I was busy caring for my mother. But I needed to enter that contest.

I looked through my story ideas, I searched the newspapers for stories, and I called family and friends asking if they had any story experiences. Nothing.

"Lord," I prayed, "I know you want me to win this contest so I can write for *Guideposts*. But I don't have a story to submit. Please send me a story."

While I waited for God's answer, I kept looking for a story. Everything came up empty. I turned the calendar to June. The contest deadline was June 16. I called more friends and family. I prayed some more. The days were eaten up by my frantic search for a story and taking care of Mom.

It was June 13. I sat in my sunny south window in the chair where I do all my reading/praying/sewing. "Lord," I prayed again. "The deadline is in three days. I can't find a story. You know I have tried. If you want me to win the contest, please send me a story."

I sat there, not having much faith that God could send me a story soon enough. I only had three days before postmark deadline. Yet I sat there, silently, waiting on God.

I waited, hands in my lap, as if to catch a story that might fall from the sky.

I waited. Mom was napping and Dave was outdoors mowing the lawn.

I sat and waited.

The phone rang. A woman's voice began talking fast, as if she was afraid she wouldn't get it all said before I hung up. "Hello, Connie. This is Karen Nelson from South Dakota. I don't know if you remember me, but I was lost in a blizzard and you wrote to me a couple years ago asking if you could interview me for a story for *Guideposts*. Well, my story has been written in all the national news magazines and I have been interviewed by all the national television shows, but no one has told my story the way

I want it told. Are you still interested in interviewing me for *Guideposts?*"

Wow!

I *knew* God answers prayers, and I *knew* God still performs miracles here on earth, but I was blown away by that phone call—giving me *exactly what I was sitting there waiting for!*

Before she finished talking, I had slid down from the seat of that chair onto my knees, thanking God for the miracle of this story.

"Can I come tomorrow?" I squeaked.

The next day was June 14, my birthday. I left early; drove to Webster, South Dakota; and interviewed Karen and her family. I stayed at a hotel, writing long into the night. The next morning I went back to ask Karen a few more questions. I drove home and finished writing the story. The next day, June 16, the postmark deadline for the contest, I drove to the post office in town and mailed my submission.

I was grateful that Karen Nelson was willing to be used for God's purpose. It evidently took a few promptings from Him while I waited for her story.

Did I win the contest? Of course I won the contest. God gave me the story that would make me a winner. I was one of fifteen winners out of 5,400 submissions. My story, "Forty Hours at Forty Below," was published in *Guideposts* magazine in December 1999.

So, since 1998, I have been part of the *Guideposts* family of writers. If you read the magazine, you have read many of my stories. Since we ghostwrite those stories, my name doesn't appear anywhere in print. Some people have told me it's unfair that I write the stories but don't get the credit. In those stories, God gets the credit, and that's the way I want it. My name appears on the check they send, and that's good enough for me. I trust God's promises in Jeremiah 29:11, *"For I know the plans I have for you," declares the LORD. "plans to prosper you and not to harm you, plans to give you hope and a future."* (NIV)

So watch for me—I'm the one "wearing purple," outrageously stepping out into a brand new future in my "mature" years, teaching people How God Speaks to Ordinary People, with more topics to come.

My Heavenly Father is not my secret anymore.

May I be a speaker at your event?

Contact Connie at 763.878.2841
or through her webpage at
www.connielounsbury.com

ABOUT THE AUTHOR

Connie Lounsbury is an author, editor, and inspirational speaker. She has a bachelor of arts degree from Metropolitan State University, St. Paul, Minnesota, and lives in rural Minnesota with her husband David. She has four daughters, eight grandchildren, and one great-grandson.

Her book, *Quit Your Job and Make Ends Meet* is out of print. Her book, *Reaching Past the Wire: A Nurse at Abu Ghraib,* was released by Borealis Books in 2007. Many short stories have been published in *Guideposts* magazines and books, as well as in other books and magazines in the United States and Japan. Numerous writing awards include First Place Award in the inspirational category of the 2001 *Writer's Digest* Writing Competition, and winner of the 1998 *Guideposts* writers contest.

Connie is a member of Faith Lutheran Church, National Association of Professional Women, American Christian Fiction Writers, Minnesota Christian Writer's Guild, The Loft Literary Center and Friends of the Library.

Her volunteer activities include Prisoner Visitation and Support Program, Share food distribution, Altar Guild and Prayer Chain coordinator.

In addition to writing and speaking, Connie likes to spend time with her family, quilt, travel, read, walk, and mentor beginning writers.

CPSIA information can be obtained at www.ICGtesting.com
Printed in the USA
BVOW010427250112

281278BV00002B/3/P